TRIANA ROBINSON

Bitcoin Unveiled

Contents

Introduction

In the early days of 2009, a new and mysterious force began to take shape in the digital ether. An enigmatic figure, known only by the pseudonym Satoshi Nakamoto, released a whitepaper outlining the concept of Bitcoin—a decentralized digital currency that promised to revolutionize the way we think about money. Since then, Bitcoin has grown from an obscure experiment into a global phenomenon, capturing the imagination of technologists, investors, and futurists alike. It has been hailed as "digital gold," a store of value for the modern age, and has been positioned by some as the future of money itself.

But as Bitcoin has risen to prominence, it has also become the center of intense debate and speculation. Is it truly the currency of the future, or is it a speculative bubble destined to burst? Who is Satoshi Nakamoto, and what are the true motivations behind Bitcoin's creation? Is Bitcoin a tool of financial liberation, or is it being manipulated by powerful forces with hidden agendas?

This book, *Bitcoin Unveiled*, aims to explore these questions and more. We will delve into the mysterious origins of Bitcoin, the myths and legends surrounding Satoshi Nakamoto, and the possibility that Bitcoin was never intended to be what it appears to be. We will examine the evolution of Bitcoin from a digital currency to "digital gold," analyzing its potential to replace traditional currencies and reshape the global financial system. And we will explore the media's role in shaping public perception of Bitcoin, questioning whether there is a coordinated effort to manipulate its image.

As Bitcoin has grown, it has attracted the attention of central banks and financial institutions around the world. Some see it as a threat to their control over the global economy, while others view it as an opportunity to create new financial instruments and markets. But what if the price of Bitcoin is being manipulated by these very institutions? Could the same entities that Bitcoin was designed to circumvent be pulling the strings behind the scenes?

In *Bitcoin Unveiled*, we will take a deep dive into the theories of central bank manipulation and the potential for Bitcoin to be co-opted by the very forces it was meant to challenge. We will also look to the future, considering what lies ahead for Bitcoin and the broader cryptocurrency market. Will Bitcoin truly become a global currency, or will it be just another chapter in the long history of financial speculation?

Throughout this book, we will explore the many facets of Bitcoin, from its mysterious beginnings to its status as a global financial power-house. We will peel back the layers of myth and media manipulation to reveal the hidden power struggles at play in the world of digital currency. Whether you are a seasoned investor, a curious technologist, or a skeptic of the cryptocurrency revolution, this book will provide you with a comprehensive understanding of the forces shaping the future of money.

As we embark on this journey together, I invite you to keep an open mind and consider the possibilities that lie ahead. Bitcoin is more than just a currency; it is a symbol of the shifting tides in the global financial landscape. What we uncover in the pages that follow may challenge your beliefs, inspire your curiosity, or even change your perspective on the future of money. Welcome to *Bitcoin Unveiled*.

1

The Genesis of Bitcoin

The year was 2008. The world was reeling from the aftershocks of one of the most devastating financial crises in modern history. Trust in traditional financial institutions was at an all-time low, as governments around the globe scrambled to stabilize economies teetering on the brink of collapse. Amidst this backdrop of uncertainty and disillusionment, a new idea was quietly taking shape—a concept that would challenge the very foundations of the global financial system.

On October 31, 2008, a whitepaper titled *"Bitcoin: A Peer-to-Peer Electronic Cash System"* was published on a cryptography mailing list. The paper was authored by a person or group of people using the pseudonym Satoshi Nakamoto. The nine-page document outlined a vision for a decentralized digital currency that would allow for peer-to-peer transactions without the need for a trusted third party, such as a bank or government. This was the birth of Bitcoin.

The Cypherpunk Movement and the Roots of Bitcoin

To understand the significance of Bitcoin's creation, it is essential to delve into the origins of the idea itself. Bitcoin did not emerge in a vacuum; it was the culmination of decades of work by a group of technologists, cryptographers, and privacy advocates who called themselves cypherpunks.

The cypherpunk movement began in the late 1980s and early 1990s, driven by the belief that privacy is a fundamental human right. These activists were deeply concerned about the growing power of governments and corporations to surveil and control individuals, particularly in the digital realm. They saw cryptography as a tool to protect personal freedoms and resist centralized control.

Among the key figures in the cypherpunk movement were individuals like David Chaum, who pioneered the concept of anonymous digital cash with his invention of DigiCash, and Nick Szabo, who developed the idea of "bit gold," a precursor to Bitcoin. These early efforts laid the groundwork for the creation of a decentralized digital currency, but none achieved widespread adoption.

Satoshi Nakamoto's whitepaper built upon these earlier ideas, solving the key problem that had plagued previous attempts at digital cash: double spending. In traditional currencies, this problem is solved by having a trusted third party, like a bank, verify transactions. But in a decentralized system with no central authority, this solution was not viable. Satoshi's innovation was the blockchain—a distributed ledger that records all transactions across a network of computers. Once a transaction is recorded on the blockchain, it cannot be altered, ensuring that each unit of Bitcoin can only be spent once.

Bitcoin's Early Days

The first Bitcoin block, known as the "genesis block," was mined by Satoshi Nakamoto on January 3, 2009. Embedded in the code of this block was a message that read, "The Times 03/Jan/2009 Chancellor on brink of second bailout for banks." This reference to a headline from The Times newspaper was widely interpreted as a commentary on the failings of the traditional financial system and a statement of purpose for Bitcoin as an alternative.

In those early days, Bitcoin was a niche project known only to a small group of cryptography enthusiasts. It had no monetary value, and there were no exchanges where it could be traded. The first Bitcoin transaction took place on May 22, 2010, when a programmer named Laszlo Hanyecz famously paid 10,000 BTC for two pizzas. At the time, this was seen as a novelty; today, those pizzas would be worth millions of dollars.

Despite its humble beginnings, Bitcoin began to gain traction among those who believed in its potential to disrupt the existing financial system. Early adopters were drawn to the idea of a currency that was not controlled by any government or central bank, and that could be transferred instantly and securely across borders without the need for intermediaries.

The Philosophy Behind Bitcoin

At its core, Bitcoin was designed as a response to the failures of the traditional financial system. The 2008 financial crisis had exposed the fragility of the global economy and the dangers of centralized control over money. Banks that were deemed "too big to fail" were bailed out with taxpayer money, while ordinary people lost their homes, savings, and livelihoods. Trust in financial institutions was shattered, and people began to question whether there was a better way.

Satoshi Nakamoto's vision for Bitcoin was rooted in the principles of decentralization, transparency, and financial sovereignty. By removing the need for a trusted third party, Bitcoin empowered individuals to take control of their own money. Transactions were verified by a network of computers (known as nodes) that operated on a consensus basis, ensuring that no single entity could manipulate the system.

Another key aspect of Bitcoin's design was its fixed supply. Unlike fiat currencies, which can be printed at will by central banks, Bitcoin has a maximum supply of 21 million coins. This scarcity is built into the protocol and is enforced by the network's consensus rules. The idea was to create a deflationary currency that would preserve its value over

5

time, unlike traditional currencies that are subject to inflation.

The Enigma of Satoshi Nakamoto

As Bitcoin began to gain attention, so did Satoshi Nakamoto. Who was this person (or group of people) who had created such revolutionary technology? Despite numerous attempts to uncover Satoshi's identity, the identity of Bitcoin's creator remains one of the greatest mysteries in the world of technology.

Various theories have been proposed over the years. Some believe that Satoshi Nakamoto is a single individual, a cryptographer or computer scientist with deep knowledge of both technology and economics. Others speculate that Satoshi is a group of people, a team of developers working together under a pseudonym. Some even suggest that Satoshi could be a government agency or an intelligence organization, using Bitcoin as an experiment in digital currency.

Satoshi Nakamoto was active in the Bitcoin community for about two years, communicating with other developers and contributing to the project's codebase. However, in 2011, Satoshi abruptly disappeared, handing over control of the Bitcoin project to other developers. In their final message, Satoshi stated, "I've moved on to other things." Since then, there has been no verified communication from Satoshi, and the identity of Bitcoin's creator remains unknown.

The Impact of Bitcoin's Mysterious Origins

The mystery surrounding Satoshi Nakamoto has had a profound impact on Bitcoin's development and its perception by the public. On one hand, the anonymity of Bitcoin's creator has contributed to the currency's allure and mystique. The idea that a decentralized currency was created by an unknown figure aligns with the principles of privacy and autonomy that Bitcoin represents.

On the other hand, the lack of knowledge about Satoshi's identity has also led to skepticism and concern. Some fear that if Satoshi's identity were to be revealed, it could have negative implications for

Bitcoin's credibility and security. For example, if Satoshi were found to be associated with a government or corporation, it could undermine the perception of Bitcoin as a truly decentralized currency.

Moreover, Satoshi Nakamoto is believed to possess a significant amount of Bitcoin—estimated to be around 1 million BTC. This represents a substantial portion of the total supply, and the potential for these coins to be moved or sold has led to speculation about their impact on the market.

The Legacy of Bitcoin's Creation

The creation of Bitcoin marked the beginning of a new era in the world of finance. It introduced the concept of a decentralized, digital currency that operates independently of traditional financial institutions and governments. The principles of transparency, security, and financial sovereignty that underpin Bitcoin have resonated with millions of people around the world, leading to its rapid adoption and growth.

However, the origins of Bitcoin are shrouded in mystery, and the identity of its creator remains unknown. This enigma has only added to Bitcoin's allure, fueling speculation and debate about the true motivations behind its creation. As we continue to explore the rise of Bitcoin in the chapters that follow, we will see how this revolutionary technology has challenged the status quo and sparked a global movement for financial freedom. But with this newfound power comes new questions: Who truly controls Bitcoin? And what role will it play in the future of money? The journey to answer these questions begins with understanding the genesis of Bitcoin—a story that is still being written.

2

Satoshi Nakamoto: The Enigma

The story of Bitcoin is inseparable from the mystery of its creator, Satoshi Nakamoto. In the annals of technological innovation, few names carry as much intrigue, speculation, and myth as Satoshi Nakamoto. The pseudonymous figure—or figures—behind Bitcoin has become a modern legend, inspiring endless debates, conspiracy theories, and quests for the truth. Despite the revolutionary impact of Bitcoin, the identity of Satoshi Nakamoto remains one of the greatest unsolved mysteries of the digital age.

The Birth of a Legend

Satoshi Nakamoto first appeared in 2008 with the publication of the Bitcoin whitepaper, a document that laid the theoretical foundation for a peer-to-peer electronic cash system. Over the next two years, Satoshi was an active participant in the early development of Bitcoin, communicating with other developers, contributing code, and refining the vision that would ultimately reshape the world of finance. However, in 2011, Satoshi abruptly withdrew from public life, leaving behind a final message: "I've moved on to other things."

This sudden disappearance only added to the mystique surrounding Satoshi. The fact that someone could create something as impactful as

Bitcoin and then vanish without a trace seemed almost unfathomable in the age of the internet, where anonymity is increasingly rare. The scarcity of information about Satoshi—no confirmed name, no verifiable location, no clear motive—has fueled countless theories about who or what Satoshi Nakamoto truly is.

Theories and Speculation

Since Satoshi's disappearance, there has been no shortage of attempts to unmask the person or group behind the pseudonym. Theories about Satoshi's identity range from the plausible to the fantastical, each with its own set of arguments and evidence. Some of the most prominent theories include:

The Lone Genius:

- One of the most popular theories is that Satoshi Nakamoto is a single individual, a brilliant cryptographer or computer scientist who single-handedly developed Bitcoin. Candidates for this theory include Nick Szabo, a computer scientist known for his work on digital currencies and smart contracts, and Hal Finney, a pioneering cryptographer who was one of the first people to work on Bitcoin's code. Both Szabo and Finney have denied being Satoshi, but their contributions to the field make them strong contenders in the eyes of many.

The Collaborative Effort:

- Another theory suggests that Satoshi Nakamoto is not an individual, but a group of people working together under a single pseudonym. This theory gains traction when considering the breadth of knowledge required to create Bitcoin—a combination of cryptography, economics, and software engineering. Some believe that Bitcoin was developed by a team of experts who chose to remain anonymous for several reasons, including fear of government backlash or simply a desire for privacy.

The Government Connection:

- Some theorists speculate that Satoshi Nakamoto could be a government agency or intelligence organization, using Bitcoin as a tool for experimentation in digital currencies or to achieve broader geopolitical objectives. This theory posits that Bitcoin might have been created to destabilize traditional financial systems, gather data on global financial transactions, or even to serve as a "honey pot" for illicit activities.

The AI Theory:

- A more outlandish theory is that Satoshi Nakamoto is not human at all, but an artificial intelligence or a collective intelligence that emerged from the internet. Proponents of this theory argue that the sophistication of Bitcoin's design, combined with the perfect anonymity of its creator, suggests something beyond human capabilities.

The Motivations Behind the Mask

While the true identity of Satoshi Nakamoto remains unknown, speculation about Satoshi's motivations is equally abundant. Understanding these motivations could provide insight into the true purpose of Bitcoin and its intended role in the world.

Privacy and Anonymity:

- One of the most straightforward explanations for Satoshi's anonymity is a desire for privacy. Bitcoin was created as a response to the centralized control of money and the erosion of individual privacy. By remaining anonymous, Satoshi may have been practicing what they preached, using the very principles of privacy and decentralization that Bitcoin was built on.

Legal and Security Concerns:

- Another possible motivation for Satoshi's anonymity is the legal and security risks associated with creating a disruptive financial technology. If Satoshi were to be identified, they could face significant legal challenges from governments and financial institutions threatened by Bitcoin. Additionally, the personal security of Satoshi could be at risk, given the vast wealth and influence Bitcoin has accumulated.

Philosophical Beliefs:

- Some believe that Satoshi's anonymity is a philosophical stance, a way to reinforce the idea that Bitcoin is a decentralized and leaderless system. By stepping away from the project and leaving it in the hands of the community, Satoshi may have been emphasizing the importance of decentralization and the power of collective ownership over a single, centralized figure.

Control and Influence:

- On the other hand, Satoshi's anonymity and disappearance could be seen as a strategic move to maintain influence over Bitcoin without direct involvement. By leaving the project, Satoshi avoided the pitfalls of power and control that often accompany revolutionary innovations. This detachment has allowed Bitcoin to evolve organically, driven by the community rather than a single leader.

The Impact of Satoshi's Disappearance

Satoshi Nakamoto's disappearance in 2011 marked a turning point for Bitcoin. Without its creator at the helm, the Bitcoin community was forced to take control of the project, leading to the decentralized development model that defines Bitcoin today. This transition from a leader-driven project to a community-driven one is one of Bitcoin's defining characteristics and has contributed to its resilience and longevity.

Decentralization and Community Ownership:

- Satoshi's disappearance underscored the importance of decentralization in Bitcoin's design. By stepping away, Satoshi ensured that no single entity would have control over Bitcoin, reinforcing the principle of distributed power. This decentralization has allowed Bitcoin to thrive in the face of external challenges, from regulatory pressures to technological threats.

The Myth and the Movement:

- Satoshi's anonymity has also contributed to the mythos of Bitcoin, turning it into more than just a currency or technology. Satoshi Nakamoto has become a symbol of the broader movement for financial sovereignty, privacy, and resistance to centralized control. This myth has galvanized supporters and fueled the spread of Bitcoin as both a financial tool and a cultural phenomenon.

The Satoshi Coins:

- One of the most significant aspects of Satoshi's legacy is the so-called "Satoshi coins"—an estimated 1 million Bitcoin that are believed to be controlled by Satoshi. These coins have never been moved or spent, leading to speculation about their fate. If these coins were ever moved, it could have a profound impact on the Bitcoin market, both in terms of price and trust. The dormant Satoshi coins serve as a constant reminder of the mystery and potential influence that Satoshi Nakamoto still holds over Bitcoin.

Satoshi's Legacy

The enigma of Satoshi Nakamoto is not just a footnote in the history of Bitcoin; it is a fundamental part of its identity. The mystery of Satoshi has helped Bitcoin transcend the realm of technology and finance, turning it into a cultural icon and a symbol of resistance against centralized power.

As Bitcoin continues to evolve and grow, the legacy of Satoshi Nakamoto will remain an enduring part of its story. Whether Satoshi was a lone genius, a group of collaborators, or something else entirely, the impact of their creation is undeniable. Bitcoin has sparked a global movement, challenging the traditional financial system and inspiring the development of countless other cryptocurrencies and blockchain technologies.

The true identity of Satoshi Nakamoto may never be revealed, and perhaps that is how it was meant to be. By remaining anonymous, Satoshi ensured that Bitcoin would not be about any one person, but about the collective power of a decentralized network. This anonymity has allowed Bitcoin to become what it is today—a force that transcends borders, governments, and individuals, and a technology that has the potential to reshape the world.

As we move forward in this exploration of Bitcoin's rise and its impact on the global financial system, the shadow of Satoshi Nakamoto will continue to loom large. The questions of who Satoshi was, why they created Bitcoin, and what their true intentions were will remain a central theme in understanding the full significance of Bitcoin in the world today.

3

Bitcoin's Evolution from Currency to Digital Gold

When Bitcoin was first introduced, it was envisioned as a revolutionary digital currency—one that could facilitate peer-to-peer transactions without the need for intermediaries like banks or payment processors. Over time, however, Bitcoin's role in the financial ecosystem has evolved, and it has come to be seen less as a day-to-day currency and more as a store of value—a new form of "digital gold." This chapter explores the factors that have driven this transformation and examines how Bitcoin's evolving identity has shaped its place in the global financial system.

The Early Vision: Bitcoin as a Digital Currency

In its original conception, Bitcoin was intended to function as a decentralized alternative to traditional currencies. Satoshi Nakamoto's whitepaper outlined a vision for a system that would allow for the direct exchange of value between individuals, free from the control of central banks and financial institutions. This was a radical idea—one that promised to disrupt the status quo and democratize access to financial services.

In the early years of Bitcoin, this vision was very much alive. Bitcoin

15

enthusiasts used the cryptocurrency to buy and sell goods and services, and a growing number of merchants began accepting Bitcoin as a form of payment. Bitcoin's low transaction fees, borderless nature, and resistance to censorship made it an attractive option for those seeking an alternative to traditional financial systems.

However, as Bitcoin gained popularity, several challenges emerged that made it difficult for the cryptocurrency to function effectively as a medium of exchange. These challenges included scalability issues, volatility, and increasing transaction costs. As Bitcoin's user base grew, the network struggled to process the increasing number of transactions, leading to delays and higher fees. Meanwhile, Bitcoin's price volatility made it difficult to use as a stable currency for everyday transactions.

The Shift Toward a Store of Value

As these challenges became more apparent, the narrative around Bitcoin began to shift. Rather than being viewed primarily as a currency, Bitcoin started to be seen as a store of value—a digital equivalent of gold. This shift was driven by several key factors:

Scarcity and Fixed Supply:

- One of the most compelling arguments for Bitcoin as a store of value is its fixed supply. Unlike fiat currencies, which can be printed in unlimited quantities by central banks, Bitcoin has a maximum supply of 21 million coins. This scarcity is built into the protocol and cannot be changed without the consensus of the entire network. As a result, Bitcoin is often compared to gold, which is also valued for its scarcity and resistance to inflation.

Decentralization and Security:

- Bitcoin's decentralized nature and strong security measures make it an attractive option for those seeking a safe haven for their wealth. Because Bitcoin transactions are recorded on a blockchain—a distributed ledger that is maintained by a global network of nodes—it is extremely difficult to tamper with or manipulate the system. This makes Bitcoin a secure store of value, particularly in comparison to fiat currencies, which are subject to the whims of central banks and governments.

Growing Institutional Interest:

- As Bitcoin's reputation as "digital gold" began to take hold, institutional investors started to take notice. Hedge funds, asset managers, and even publicly traded companies began to allocate a portion of their portfolios to Bitcoin, viewing it as a hedge against inflation and economic uncertainty. This influx of institutional capital further solidified Bitcoin's status as a store of value and contributed to its rising price.

Bitcoin as a Hedge Against Economic Uncertainty:

- The global financial crises of the 21st century, from the 2008 meltdown to the economic disruptions caused by the COVID-19 pandemic, have underscored the vulnerabilities of traditional financial systems. In this context, Bitcoin has emerged as a hedge against economic uncertainty, offering a decentralized and apolitical alternative to fiat currencies that are susceptible to inflation, currency devaluation, and government intervention.

Bitcoin vs. Gold: A New Kind of Safe Haven

As Bitcoin's role as a store of value has become more prominent, comparisons to gold have become increasingly common. Both assets are seen as "safe havens"—investments that can preserve wealth in times of economic turmoil. However, there are important differences between the two that have led to ongoing debate about whether Bitcoin can truly replace gold as the ultimate store of value.

Portability and Divisibility:

- One of Bitcoin's key advantages over gold is its portability. Unlike gold, which is heavy and difficult to transport, Bitcoin can be easily transferred across the globe in a matter of minutes. Additionally, Bitcoin is highly divisible, with each coin being divisible into 100 million smaller units (known as satoshis). This makes it possible to transact in very small amounts, which is not practical with physical gold.

Digital Nature and Accessibility:

- Bitcoin's digital nature also makes it more accessible to a broader range of people. Anyone with an internet connection can buy, sell, or store Bitcoin, regardless of their location or financial status. This stands in contrast to gold, which requires physical storage and is often subject to regulatory restrictions.

Volatility and Market Maturity:

- Despite its many advantages, Bitcoin's volatility remains a significant challenge to its status as a store of value. While gold has been used as a store of value for thousands of years and has a relatively stable price, Bitcoin's price can fluctuate dramatically over short periods of time. This volatility has led some to question whether Bitcoin can truly serve as a reliable store of value, especially in the face of market speculation and manipulation.

Emerging Narratives and Adoption:

- As Bitcoin continues to gain acceptance and adoption, its narrative as a store of value has strengthened. Major financial institutions, corporations, and even governments are beginning to recognize Bitcoin as a legitimate asset class, and this growing institutional interest is helping to stabilize its price. However, the debate over whether Bitcoin can truly replace gold as the ultimate store of value is far from settled.

The Implications of Bitcoin's Evolution

The evolution of Bitcoin from a digital currency to a store of value has had significant implications for its role in the global financial system. As Bitcoin has become more widely accepted as "digital gold," its use as a medium of exchange has diminished. Today, Bitcoin is primarily seen as an investment asset—a way to preserve and grow wealth in the face of economic uncertainty.

Impact on Adoption and Use Cases:

- As Bitcoin's narrative has shifted, so too have its use cases. While Bitcoin was initially promoted as a means of facilitating everyday transactions, its use for this purpose has declined. Instead, Bitcoin is now primarily used as a long-term investment, a hedge against inflation, and a tool for wealth preservation. This shift has led to the rise of other cryptocurrencies, such as Ethereum, which are better suited for day-to-day transactions and smart contracts.

Regulatory and Institutional Responses:

- The growing perception of Bitcoin as a store of value has also attracted the attention of regulators and financial institutions.

Governments around the world are grappling with how to regulate Bitcoin, particularly in light of its increasing institutional adoption. Meanwhile, traditional financial institutions are exploring ways to integrate Bitcoin into their offerings, from Bitcoin ETFs to custody services for institutional investors.

The Future of Bitcoin as a Store of Value:

- Looking ahead, the question remains whether Bitcoin will continue to evolve as a store of value or whether it will reclaim its original role as a digital currency. As the Bitcoin network undergoes technological upgrades, such as the implementation of the Lightning Network for faster transactions, there is potential for Bitcoin to become more widely used as a medium of exchange. However, its status as "digital gold" is likely to remain a key part of its identity for the foreseeable future.

A New Financial Paradigm

Bitcoin's evolution from a digital currency to a store of value represents a fundamental shift in how it is perceived and used. While it may have started as a way to facilitate peer-to-peer transactions, Bitcoin has become something much more—a new kind of asset that offers a decentralized, secure, and apolitical alternative to traditional stores of value like gold.

As we continue to explore Bitcoin's role in the global financial system, it is clear that its impact extends far beyond its original purpose. Bitcoin has sparked a new financial paradigm, challenging the status quo and offering a glimpse of a future where money is not controlled by governments or central banks, but by the people who use it. Whether Bitcoin will ultimately fulfill this vision remains to be seen, but its journey from digital currency to digital gold is a testament to its resilience and its potential to reshape the world of finance.

4

Positioning Bitcoin as a Global Currency

As Bitcoin has evolved from a digital currency to a store of value, the idea of it becoming a global currency has captured the imagination of both its supporters and skeptics. The potential for Bitcoin to replace or coexist with traditional fiat currencies in the global financial system is a topic of intense debate. This chapter explores the various factors that have positioned Bitcoin as a candidate for global currency status, the challenges it faces in achieving this role, and the implications of such a shift for the world economy.

The Global Appeal of Bitcoin

Bitcoin's decentralized nature and borderless design make it inherently global. Unlike fiat currencies, which are tied to specific nations and subject to government policies, Bitcoin operates independently of any central authority. This has led to its adoption in countries around the world, particularly in regions where the local currency is unstable or where access to traditional financial services is limited.

Bitcoin as a Solution to Hyperinflation and Currency Devaluation:

- In countries experiencing hyperinflation or severe currency devaluation, Bitcoin has been embraced as a hedge against the erosion of wealth. For example, in countries like Venezuela and Zimbabwe, where hyperinflation has rendered the national currency nearly worthless, Bitcoin provides a way for citizens to preserve value and conduct transactions in a more stable currency.

The Role of Remittances and Cross-Border Payments:

- Bitcoin's ability to facilitate low-cost, fast cross-border transactions has made it a popular choice for remittances. In many developing countries, remittances from family members working abroad are a crucial source of income. Traditional remittance services often charge high fees and can take days to process transactions. Bitcoin offers a cheaper and faster alternative, allowing for the near-instant transfer of funds across borders without the need for intermediaries.

Financial Inclusion and Access:

- In regions where access to banking services is limited, Bitcoin offers a way for individuals to participate in the global economy. With just a smartphone and an internet connection, anyone can send, receive, and store Bitcoin, bypassing the need for a traditional bank account. This has significant implications for financial inclusion, particularly in developing countries where large portions of the population are unbanked.

Challenges to Bitcoin as a Global Currency

While Bitcoin's global reach and decentralized nature make it a strong candidate for a global currency, several significant challenges must be overcome for it to fulfill this role. These challenges include scalability issues, volatility, regulatory uncertainty, and the need for broader adoption and acceptance.

Scalability and Transaction Speed:

- One of the most significant technical challenges facing Bitcoin is scalability. As the network grows, the number of transactions that can be processed per second is limited by the block size and the time it takes to confirm transactions. During periods of high demand, this can lead to delays and higher transaction fees, making Bitcoin less practical for everyday transactions. Solutions like the Lightning Network, which enables faster and cheaper transactions by processing them off-chain, are being developed to address these issues, but widespread adoption of these solutions is still in progress.

Volatility and Price Stability:

- Bitcoin's price volatility is another major obstacle to its use as a global currency. While volatility can attract speculative investment, it makes Bitcoin less suitable for use in everyday transactions, where price stability is essential. A merchant, for example, needs to be confident that the value of the Bitcoin they receive for goods or services will not fluctuate dramatically by the time they convert it into their local currency. Stablecoins, which are pegged to the value of traditional currencies, have emerged as a potential solution to this issue, but Bitcoin's inherent volatility remains a challenge.

Regulatory Uncertainty:

- The regulatory environment for Bitcoin varies widely from country to country, creating uncertainty for users and businesses. Some governments have embraced Bitcoin, while others have banned or heavily restricted its use. The lack of a consistent regulatory framework makes it difficult for Bitcoin to gain widespread acceptance as a global currency. Furthermore, governments may resist the adoption of Bitcoin as a global currency, seeing it as a threat to their control over monetary policy and economic stability.

Adoption and Integration:

- For Bitcoin to function as a global currency, it must be widely accepted by both individuals and businesses. While Bitcoin's adoption has grown significantly, it is still far from universal. Many people are unfamiliar with how to use Bitcoin, and many businesses do not accept it as a form of payment. For Bitcoin to achieve global currency status, there needs to be greater education, infrastructure development, and integration with existing financial systems.

The Role of Institutional Adoption

The involvement of institutional players in the Bitcoin ecosystem has been a significant factor in its growing acceptance and legitimacy. As more financial institutions, corporations, and even governments begin to embrace Bitcoin, its potential to function as a global currency becomes more plausible.

Corporations Embracing Bitcoin:

- Several major corporations have begun to accept Bitcoin as payment for goods and services, while others have added Bitcoin to their balance sheets as a reserve asset. Companies like Tesla, MicroStrategy, and Square have made headlines for their significant Bitcoin holdings, signaling confidence in Bitcoin's long-term value. This corporate adoption not only helps to stabilize the market but also increases Bitcoin's visibility and legitimacy as a global currency.

Financial Institutions and Bitcoin:

- Traditional financial institutions, including banks, asset managers, and payment processors, are increasingly integrating Bitcoin into their offerings. Bitcoin exchange-traded funds (ETFs), custody services, and Bitcoin-backed loans are just a few examples of how the financial industry is adapting to the growing demand for Bitcoin. As these institutions build infrastructure around Bitcoin, they help bridge the gap between the traditional financial system and the emerging world of digital currencies.

Government Interest and Regulation:

- Governments are also starting to take Bitcoin more seriously, with some even exploring the possibility of integrating Bitcoin into their national financial systems. El Salvador made headlines in 2021 when it became the first country to adopt Bitcoin as legal tender, allowing citizens to use Bitcoin for everyday transactions and requiring businesses to accept it alongside the U.S. dollar. While El Salvador's experiment is still in its early stages, it has sparked interest in other countries considering similar moves.

The Role of Central Bank Digital Currencies (CBDCs):

- The rise of Bitcoin has prompted central banks to explore the development of their own digital currencies, known as Central Bank Digital Currencies (CBDCs). While CBDCs are fundamentally different from Bitcoin in that they are centralized and issued by governments, they represent a significant shift in the way money is conceptualized and used. The development of CBDCs could either complement or compete with Bitcoin, depending on how they are implemented and adopted.

Scenarios for Bitcoin as a Global Currency

As Bitcoin continues to gain traction, several potential scenarios could unfold in its journey toward becoming a global currency. These scenarios range from Bitcoin fully replacing traditional fiat currencies to a more integrated financial system where Bitcoin coexists with other forms of money.

Bitcoin as a Parallel Currency:

- In this scenario, Bitcoin coexists alongside traditional fiat currencies, with individuals and businesses choosing to use Bitcoin for certain transactions while still relying on fiat currencies for others. This could lead to a dual monetary system where Bitcoin is used for cross-border transactions, savings, and investment, while fiat currencies remain dominant for everyday spending.

Bitcoin as the Dominant Global Currency:

- In a more extreme scenario, Bitcoin could eventually replace traditional fiat currencies as the dominant form of money in the global economy. This would require widespread adoption, significant advancements in scalability and price stability, and a shift in how governments and financial institutions approach monetary policy. While this scenario may seem far-fetched, it is not entirely out of the realm of possibility, especially in a world where trust in traditional financial systems continues to erode.

Bitcoin as a Reserve Currency:

- Another potential scenario is for Bitcoin to become a global reserve currency, similar to the role that gold has played historically. In this scenario, governments and central banks could hold Bitcoin as part of their foreign exchange reserves, using it to back their national currencies and stabilize their economies. This would position Bitcoin as a key component of the global financial system, even if it is not used for everyday transactions by individuals.

Bitcoin as a Niche Asset:

- Finally, it is possible that Bitcoin remains a niche asset, used primarily by investors and enthusiasts rather than becoming a mainstream global currency. In this scenario, Bitcoin's role as "digital gold" would continue to grow, but it would not achieve widespread adoption as a medium of exchange. Instead, other cryptocurrencies or digital currencies, such as CBDCs, might fill the role of a global currency.

The Implications of a Bitcoin-Dominated World

If Bitcoin were to achieve global currency status, the implications for the world economy would be profound. A Bitcoin-dominated financial system would represent a significant departure from the current model, with potential benefits and risks.

Decentralization of Power:

- One of the most significant implications of a Bitcoin-dominated world is the decentralization of financial power. In such a system, control over money would shift from governments and central banks to a decentralized network of users. This could lead to greater financial freedom and autonomy for individuals but could also weaken the ability of governments to implement monetary policy and respond to economic crises.

Impact on Global Trade and Finance:

- A global currency like Bitcoin could simplify international trade and finance by eliminating the need for currency exchange and reducing transaction costs. However, it could also lead to greater volatility in global markets, particularly if Bitcoin's price remains unstable. Additionally, countries that rely on monetary policy to manage their economies could face challenges in a world where Bitcoin is the dominant currency.

Social and Economic Inequality:

- The widespread adoption of Bitcoin as a global currency could have mixed effects on social and economic inequality. On one hand, Bitcoin's decentralized nature could empower individuals in developing countries and those without access to traditional banking services. On the other hand, the early adopters of Bitcoin, who have accumulated significant wealth, could see their influence and power grow, potentially exacerbating existing inequalities.

Environmental Considerations:

- The environmental impact of Bitcoin mining is another critical consideration. Bitcoin's proof-of-work consensus mechanism requires significant energy consumption, leading to concerns about its sustainability as a global currency. If Bitcoin were to achieve widespread adoption, there would likely be increased pressure to transition to more energy-efficient technologies or to find ways to mitigate the environmental impact of mining.

The Road Ahead

Bitcoin's journey toward becoming a global currency is far from certain, but its potential to reshape the global financial system cannot be ignored. As we explore the various scenarios and challenges associated with Bitcoin's evolution, it is clear that the world is at a crossroads. The decisions made by governments, financial institutions, and individuals in the coming years will determine whether Bitcoin remains a niche asset, becomes a parallel currency, or achieves its full potential as a dominant global currency.

The road ahead is filled with challenges, but it is also full of opportunities. Bitcoin's decentralized nature, global reach, and growing acceptance position it as a powerful force in the ongoing evolution of money. Whether it ultimately becomes a global currency or not, Bitcoin has already left an indelible mark on the world of finance, sparking a revolution that shows no signs of slowing down. As we continue to witness the unfolding of this revolution, one thing is certain: the future of money will never be the same.

5

The Power of Media: Shaping Bitcoin's Image

As Bitcoin has evolved from an obscure digital experiment to a global financial phenomenon, the role of the media in shaping its image has been both significant and complex. The media has the power to influence public perception, drive market sentiment, and ultimately affect the adoption and value of Bitcoin. In this chapter, we will explore how the media has portrayed Bitcoin over the years, the narratives that have emerged, and the impact these narratives have had on Bitcoin's development and acceptance.

The Early Days: Skepticism and Dismissal

In the early years of Bitcoin, mainstream media coverage was sparse and often dismissive. Bitcoin was largely seen as a fringe project, associated with tech enthusiasts, libertarians, and cypherpunks. The media narrative during this period was characterized by skepticism and a general lack of understanding of the technology and its potential.

The "Magic Internet Money" Narrative:

- One of the earliest and most pervasive media narratives was that Bitcoin was little more than "magic internet money"—a curious but ultimately trivial experiment in digital currency. Articles often highlighted the novelty of Bitcoin but downplayed its potential as a serious financial asset. This narrative was fueled by the fact that Bitcoin had no intrinsic value, was not backed by any government or physical asset, and was used by a relatively small community of users.

Associations with Illicit Activities:

- Another common theme in early media coverage was the association of Bitcoin with illicit activities, particularly on the dark web. The infamous Silk Road marketplace, which operated from 2011 to 2013, allowed users to buy and sell illegal goods and services using Bitcoin. This association led to negative headlines and further skepticism about Bitcoin's legitimacy. Many articles framed Bitcoin as a tool for criminals, reinforcing the idea that it was not suitable for mainstream adoption.

The Shift to Curiosity and Interest

As Bitcoin continued to grow and attract more users, the media's tone began to shift from outright skepticism to curiosity and cautious interest. This period was marked by a growing recognition of Bitcoin's potential, even if it was still viewed with a degree of caution.

The Emergence of Bitcoin Millionaires:

- One of the key factors that contributed to this shift was the emergence of early Bitcoin adopters who became millionaires as the price of Bitcoin skyrocketed. Stories of individuals who had bought Bitcoin for a few cents or dollars and then sold it for thousands captured the public's imagination and helped to legitimize Bitcoin as an investment. Media outlets began to cover these success stories, highlighting the potential for significant financial gains.

The Technology Behind Bitcoin:

- Another factor that contributed to the media's growing interest in Bitcoin was the recognition of the technology behind it—particularly blockchain technology. As more people began to understand the potential applications of blockchain beyond just digital currency, media coverage started to focus on the innovation and possibilities that Bitcoin represented. This shift in focus helped to broaden the conversation about Bitcoin and introduced the concept to a wider audience.

Institutional Interest and Mainstream Coverage:

- As institutional interest in Bitcoin began to grow, so too did mainstream media coverage. Financial news outlets like Bloomberg, CNBC, and The Wall Street Journal started to cover Bitcoin more regularly, treating it as a legitimate asset class. This coverage brought Bitcoin into the mainstream financial conversation and helped to further legitimize it in the eyes of both investors and the general public.

The Boom and Bust Cycles: Media's Role in Market Sentiment

One of the most significant ways the media has influenced Bitcoin is through its coverage of the boom and bust cycles that have characterized Bitcoin's price history. These cycles have been marked by periods of intense media attention, followed by equally intense scrutiny and negative coverage during downturns.

The 2013 Bull Run and Subsequent Crash:

- Bitcoin's first major bull run in 2013 saw its price rise from around $100 to over $1,000 in a matter of months. This meteoric rise attracted significant media attention, with headlines proclaiming the arrival of a new financial era. However, when the price subsequently crashed, much of the media coverage turned negative, with articles questioning whether Bitcoin was a bubble or a scam. This pattern of hype followed by skepticism would become a recurring theme in Bitcoin's media narrative.

The 2017-2018 Bull Run and Crash:

- The 2017 bull run was another pivotal moment in Bitcoin's history, with the price reaching nearly $20,000 by the end of the year. Media coverage during this period was intense, with daily stories about Bitcoin's price movements, new investors entering the market, and the growing interest in Initial Coin Offerings (ICOs). However, when the bubble burst in early 2018 and Bitcoin's price plummeted, the media once again turned negative, with headlines declaring the "death" of Bitcoin and warning of the dangers of speculative investment.

The Role of Media in Amplifying Volatility:

- The media's focus on Bitcoin's price movements has played a significant role in amplifying its volatility. Positive coverage during bull runs can create a feedback loop, where increased attention drives more investment, leading to higher prices and more coverage. Conversely, negative coverage during downturns can exacerbate panic selling, driving prices down further and reinforcing the negative narrative. This dynamic has made it difficult for Bitcoin to shed its image as a volatile and risky asset.

Media Narratives and Public Perception

The media's portrayal of Bitcoin has not only influenced market sentiment but also shaped public perception of what Bitcoin is and what it represents. Different narratives have emerged over time, each contributing to how Bitcoin is understood by the broader public.

Bitcoin as Digital Gold:

- One of the most enduring media narratives is the comparison of Bitcoin to gold. This narrative positions Bitcoin as a store of value, a hedge against inflation, and a "safe haven" asset in times of economic uncertainty. The "digital gold" narrative has been particularly influential in attracting institutional investors and has helped to legitimize Bitcoin as a long-term investment.

Bitcoin as a Bubble:

- The narrative of Bitcoin as a speculative bubble has also been a recurring theme in media coverage. This narrative focuses on the extreme volatility of Bitcoin's price, the risks associated with investing in it, and the possibility that it could all come crashing down. While this narrative has been less prominent during bull markets, it resurfaces whenever Bitcoin's price experiences significant declines.

Bitcoin as a Tool for Criminals:

- Despite the growing acceptance of Bitcoin, the narrative that it is primarily used for illicit activities has persisted in some corners of the media. This narrative is often tied to stories about dark web marketplaces, ransomware attacks, and money laundering. While the reality is that Bitcoin is used for a wide range of legitimate purposes, the association with criminal activity continues to shape public perception.

Bitcoin as a Financial Revolution:

- Another powerful narrative that has emerged is the idea of Bitcoin as a financial revolution—a technology that has the potential to disrupt the traditional financial system and empower individuals. This narrative has been particularly resonant with those who are disillusioned with banks, governments, and the status quo. It positions Bitcoin as a tool for financial sovereignty and democratization, aligning it with broader social and political movements.

The Influence of Social Media and Independent Voices

While traditional media has played a significant role in shaping Bitcoin's image, the rise of social media and independent content creators has introduced new dynamics to the conversation. Platforms like Twitter, Reddit, YouTube, and podcasts have become important venues for discussions about Bitcoin, allowing for a more decentralized and diverse range of voices to influence public perception.

The Role of Twitter and Reddit:

- Twitter has become a key platform for the Bitcoin community, where influencers, developers, investors, and enthusiasts share news, insights, and opinions in real-time. Hashtags like #Bitcoin and #HODL (Hold On for Dear Life) have become rallying cries for the community, while accounts with large followings can move markets with a single tweet. Reddit, particularly the subreddit r/Bitcoin, has also been instrumental in fostering discussion and debate, providing a forum for both seasoned veterans and newcomers to share knowledge and experiences.

YouTube and Podcasts:

- YouTube and podcasts have provided platforms for in-depth discussions about Bitcoin, offering everything from technical analysis to interviews with industry leaders. Influential YouTubers and podcasters have built large audiences, often serving as trusted sources of information for their followers. These independent content creators have helped to democratize access to information about Bitcoin, allowing people to learn about it outside the traditional media framework.

The Power of Memes and Internet Culture:

- Memes and internet culture have also played a unique role in shaping the public perception of Bitcoin. Concepts like "HODL," "To the Moon," and "Bitcoin Maximalism" have become part of the Bitcoin lexicon, reinforcing the community's identity and shared values. These cultural artifacts, often spread through social media, help to make Bitcoin more relatable and accessible, particularly to younger generations.

The Media's Role in Bitcoin's Future

As Bitcoin continues to evolve, the media's role in shaping its image will remain crucial. How Bitcoin is portrayed in the media will influence not only public perception but also regulatory decisions, institutional adoption, and market dynamics. The narratives that dominate the media landscape will play a significant role in determining Bitcoin's future trajectory.

Balancing Hype with Reality:

- One of the challenges for the media going forward will be balancing the hype around Bitcoin with a more nuanced understanding of its risks and potential. As Bitcoin becomes more integrated into the global financial system, media coverage will need to evolve to reflect its growing maturity and complexity. This will require a shift away from sensationalism and towards more informed and balanced reporting.

Addressing Misconceptions:

- The media also has a responsibility to address misconceptions about Bitcoin, particularly those that persist from its early days. As the technology and use cases for Bitcoin continue to develop, it will be important for the media to provide accurate and up-to-date information that reflects the current state of the industry. This includes correcting outdated narratives about Bitcoin's association with criminal activity and highlighting its legitimate uses.

The Impact of New Media Forms:

- As new forms of media continue to emerge, the influence of traditional media on Bitcoin may diminish. Decentralized platforms, blockchain-based social networks, and other innovations could reshape how information about Bitcoin is disseminated and consumed. The rise of independent content creators and social media influencers suggests that the future of Bitcoin's image may be shaped more by the community itself than by traditional media gatekeepers.

The Power of Perception
The media has played a pivotal role in shaping the public's understanding of Bitcoin, influencing its adoption, market behavior, and overall

narrative. From the early days of skepticism and dismissal to the more recent focus on Bitcoin as "digital gold," the media's portrayal of Bitcoin has evolved in response to its growing prominence and complexity.

As Bitcoin continues to challenge the status quo and carve out its place in the global financial system, the power of perception will remain a key factor in its success or failure. Whether Bitcoin is ultimately seen as a revolutionary technology, a speculative asset, or something in between will depend in large part on the narratives that dominate the media landscape. As we move forward, the ongoing dialogue between Bitcoin and the media will be crucial in shaping the future of money and finance.

6

The Conspiracy of Media Manipulation

The power of media to shape public perception and influence market behavior is undeniable, especially in the context of Bitcoin. While the previous chapter explored the general evolution of media narratives around Bitcoin, this chapter delves into a more controversial and complex aspect: the possibility that the media's portrayal of Bitcoin has been manipulated by powerful entities with vested interests. From coordinated efforts to suppress Bitcoin's image to strategic hype cycles, we will examine the theories and evidence suggesting that Bitcoin's media coverage may not always be as impartial as it seems.

The Case for Media Manipulation

Media manipulation is not a new phenomenon; it has been a tool of influence used by governments, corporations, and other powerful groups throughout history. In the case of Bitcoin, which poses a significant challenge to the traditional financial system, the stakes are particularly high. If Bitcoin succeeds in its potential to decentralize money and empower individuals, it could disrupt the control that governments and financial institutions have over the global economy. This potential threat has led some to speculate that there are coordinated efforts to manipulate the media's portrayal of Bitcoin in order to

THE CONSPIRACY OF MEDIA MANIPULATION

maintain the status quo.

Protecting the Traditional Financial System:

- One of the primary motivations for media manipulation could be the desire to protect the traditional financial system. Banks, central banks, and financial institutions have long been the gatekeepers of the global economy, and the rise of Bitcoin represents a direct challenge to their authority. By influencing media coverage to downplay Bitcoin's legitimacy or highlight its risks, these entities could be attempting to slow its adoption and maintain control over the financial system.

Suppressing Public Confidence in Bitcoin:

- Another possible motivation is the desire to suppress public confidence in Bitcoin. If the general public views Bitcoin as risky, unstable, or associated with criminal activity, they are less likely to adopt it as a currency or investment. Media narratives that focus on Bitcoin's volatility, its use in illicit activities, or its speculative nature can contribute to a climate of fear and uncertainty, deterring potential users and investors.

Strategic Timing of Negative Coverage:

- There is also the theory that negative media coverage of Bitcoin is strategically timed to coincide with key market events. For example, during periods of significant price increases, negative stories may be released to trigger panic selling and drive the price down. Conversely, during market downturns, positive coverage may be used to encourage buying and stabilize the market. This type of manipulation could be carried out by large financial institutions or "whales" (individuals or entities that hold large amounts of Bitcoin) who stand to benefit from price fluctuations.

Examples of Potential Media Manipulation

While concrete evidence of coordinated media manipulation is difficult to obtain, there are several instances where the timing and content of media coverage have raised suspicions among Bitcoin advocates and analysts.

The 2017-2018 Bitcoin Bubble:

- During the 2017 Bitcoin bull run, media coverage of Bitcoin was overwhelmingly positive, with headlines proclaiming the dawn of a new financial era. However, as the price reached its peak, a wave of negative coverage followed, focusing on the risks of a speculative bubble and the potential for a massive crash. When the price did crash in early 2018, the negative coverage intensified, with some outlets declaring the "death" of Bitcoin. The abrupt shift in tone led some to speculate that the media was being used to manipulate market sentiment, either by influencing retail investors or by aiding large players in exiting the market at peak prices.

Regulatory Announcements and Media Coverage:

- Another example of potential media manipulation is the coverage of regulatory announcements related to Bitcoin. In some cases, negative news about potential government crackdowns on Bitcoin has coincided with significant price drops, leading to speculation that such news is strategically timed. For instance, when China announced crackdowns on Bitcoin mining and trading in 2021, there was a noticeable impact on the market. The timing and framing of these announcements in the media led some to believe that they were part of a coordinated effort to suppress Bitcoin's price and slow its adoption.

The Influence of Financial Media:

- Financial media outlets, which have significant influence over investor sentiment, have also been scrutinized for their coverage of Bitcoin. Some analysts argue that these outlets, which often have close ties to traditional financial institutions, may be biased in their reporting on Bitcoin. For example, prominent financial analysts who have previously worked for major banks or investment firms may have a vested interest in portraying Bitcoin in a negative light. This could lead to a disproportionate focus on Bitcoin's risks and downplay its potential benefits.

The Role of Social Media and Independent Media in Countering Manipulation

While traditional media has a significant influence on public perception of Bitcoin, the rise of social media and independent media outlets has provided a counterbalance to potential manipulation. These platforms allow for a more diverse range of voices and perspectives, making it more difficult for any single entity to control the narrative.

Social Media as a Decentralized Information Source:

- Social media platforms like Twitter, Reddit, and YouTube have become important sources of information and discussion about Bitcoin. Unlike traditional media, which is often controlled by a few large corporations, social media is decentralized and allows for a wider range of opinions and analysis. This decentralization makes it more difficult for coordinated efforts to manipulate the narrative, as independent voices can challenge misleading or biased reporting.

The Rise of Bitcoin Influencers:

- Another important development is the rise of Bitcoin influencers—individuals who have built large followings on social media and independent media platforms. These influencers often provide analysis, news, and commentary on Bitcoin, offering alternative perspectives to those presented in traditional media. Because they are not tied to traditional financial institutions or media corporations, these influencers can offer more objective and often more informed views on Bitcoin.

Community-Driven Media Initiatives:

- The Bitcoin community has also taken steps to create its own media outlets, podcasts, and blogs that focus on providing accurate and balanced information about Bitcoin. These community-driven initiatives are often funded by donations or through decentralized models, ensuring that they remain independent from traditional financial interests. By creating their own media channels, Bitcoin advocates can counteract potential manipulation and ensure that alternative narratives are available to the public.

Assessing the Evidence: Is Media Manipulation Real?

While the theory of media manipulation in the context of Bitcoin is compelling, it is important to approach the topic with a critical eye. The lack of concrete evidence makes it difficult to definitively prove that media manipulation is taking place, and there are alternative explanations for the patterns observed in media coverage.

Market Dynamics and Media Sensationalism:

- One alternative explanation is that the patterns observed in Bitcoin's media coverage are simply a result of market dynamics and media sensationalism. Bitcoin's price volatility makes it a natural target for sensational headlines, and the media's focus on dramatic stories can amplify market movements. In this view, the media is not necessarily being manipulated, but rather is responding to the natural ebb and flow of market sentiment.

The Role of Cognitive Biases:

- Another explanation is that cognitive biases, such as confirmation bias and recency bias, play a role in how people perceive media coverage of Bitcoin. For example, during a bull market, positive news may be more likely to be shared and discussed, reinforcing the perception of media hype. Conversely, during a bear market, negative news may be more salient, leading to the perception that the media is overly pessimistic. These biases can contribute to the belief that the media is being manipulated, even if the coverage is simply reflecting broader market trends.

The Complexity of Bitcoin's Narrative:

- Bitcoin is a complex and multifaceted phenomenon, and its media narrative reflects this complexity. The fact that Bitcoin can be simultaneously viewed as a revolutionary technology, a speculative asset, a risky investment, and a tool for criminals makes it difficult for the media to present a consistent narrative. This complexity can lead to the perception of manipulation, as different outlets or analysts may focus on different aspects of Bitcoin's story.

The Impact of Media Manipulation on Bitcoin's Future

Whether or not media manipulation is taking place, the perception of manipulation itself can have significant consequences for Bitcoin's future. If people believe that the media is being manipulated to suppress Bitcoin, it could lead to increased skepticism of traditional media outlets and a greater reliance on alternative sources of information. This could further decentralize the flow of information about Bitcoin and strengthen the role of independent media.

The Role of Trust in Media and Institutions:

- Trust is a crucial factor in the adoption of any new technology, and Bitcoin is no exception. If people believe that the media is being manipulated to portray Bitcoin in a negative light, it could erode trust in traditional media and financial institutions. This could lead to a greater embrace of Bitcoin as a decentralized alternative to the current system, particularly among those who are already disillusioned with traditional institutions.

The Potential for Backlash Against Manipulation:

- If evidence of media manipulation were to emerge, it could trigger a backlash against those responsible. This could lead to increased regulatory scrutiny of media practices and a push for greater transparency in how Bitcoin is covered. It could also galvanize the Bitcoin community to take more proactive steps in countering negative narratives and promoting accurate information about the technology.

The Long-Term Impact on Bitcoin's Adoption:

- Ultimately, the way Bitcoin is portrayed in the media will play a significant role in its long-term adoption. If media manipulation is successful in suppressing Bitcoin's image, it could slow its growth and limit its acceptance as a mainstream currency or asset. Conversely, if Bitcoin's advocates are successful in countering negative narratives and promoting its benefits, it could accelerate its adoption and solidify its place in the global financial system.

Navigating the Media Landscape

The media's role in shaping the narrative around Bitcoin is a powerful force, capable of influencing public perception, market behavior, and regulatory decisions. While the evidence of media manipulation is not conclusive, the possibility that powerful entities are attempting to influence the narrative should not be dismissed.

As Bitcoin continues to evolve and challenge the traditional financial system, it is likely that the media's portrayal of Bitcoin will remain a battleground. Navigating this complex media landscape requires a critical approach, an awareness of potential biases, and a willingness to seek out diverse perspectives. Whether through traditional media, social media, or independent voices, the narratives that emerge around Bitcoin will play a crucial role in determining its future in the global economy.

7

Central Banks and the Threat of Bitcoin

As Bitcoin has grown in prominence, it has increasingly come under the scrutiny of central banks around the world. Bitcoin's decentralized nature and its potential to disrupt traditional financial systems pose a significant challenge to the authority and control of these institutions. In this chapter, we will explore why central banks view Bitcoin as a threat, how they have responded to its rise, and the ongoing struggle between decentralized digital currencies and centralized financial power.

The Role of Central Banks in the Global Economy

To understand why central banks, perceive Bitcoin as a threat, it is essential first to understand the role these institutions play in the global economy. Central banks are responsible for managing a country's monetary policy, which includes controlling inflation, regulating the money supply, setting interest rates, and maintaining the stability of the financial system. They also play a key role in issuing and managing the national currency.

Central banks exert major influence over the economy by adjusting interest rates to control inflation and by using tools like quantitative easing to manage economic growth. By controlling the money supply, central banks can influence everything from the cost of borrowing to the value of the currency on international markets. This central control has been a cornerstone of modern economic policy, and any challenge to it is seen as a potential threat to economic stability.

Why Bitcoin Threatens Central Banks

Bitcoin represents a fundamental challenge to the traditional role of central banks in several keyways:

Decentralization:

- Unlike traditional currencies, which are issued and regulated by central banks, Bitcoin is decentralized and operates on a peer-to-peer network. This means that no single entity, including central banks, has control over Bitcoin's issuance, supply, or transactions. This lack of central control is antithetical to the way central banks manage traditional currencies and could undermine their ability to implement monetary policy effectively.

Fixed Supply and Inflation Control:

- One of the primary tools central banks use to manage inflation is adjusting the money supply. When inflation is high, central banks can raise interest rates or reduce the money supply to cool the economy. Conversely, they can lower interest rates or increase the money supply to stimulate growth. Bitcoin's fixed supply of 21 million coins, which cannot be altered, removes this lever from the hands of central banks. If Bitcoin were to become widely adopted as a currency, central banks would lose a critical tool for managing the economy.

Competition with National Currencies:

- As Bitcoin gains acceptance, it has the potential to compete with national currencies, particularly in countries with unstable or devalued currencies. If citizens start using Bitcoin instead of their local currency, it could weaken the demand for the national currency, leading to its devaluation and a loss of control for the central bank. This scenario is particularly concerning for countries facing economic instability, where Bitcoin could be seen as a more stable alternative to the national currency.

Challenges to Financial Surveillance:

- Central banks, in coordination with governments, often use financial surveillance to monitor transactions, prevent money laundering, and enforce economic sanctions. Bitcoin's pseudonymous nature and decentralized network make it more difficult for authorities to track and control transactions. While Bitcoin transactions are recorded on a public ledger, the identities of the parties involved are not always easily traceable, which can hinder the ability of central banks to enforce financial regulations.

Central Bank Responses to Bitcoin

Given the potential threat that Bitcoin poses to their authority, central banks have responded in many ways. These responses range from outright hostility to cautious acceptance and even efforts to co-opt the technology behind Bitcoin.

Outright Bans and Restrictions:

- Some central banks have taken a hardline approach to Bitcoin by implementing outright bans or severe restrictions on its use. For example, in countries like China, the government has banned financial institutions from handling Bitcoin transactions and has cracked down on Bitcoin mining operations. These measures are aimed at curbing the influence of Bitcoin and preventing it from undermining the national currency and financial system.

Regulatory Measures and Warnings:

• Other central banks have not gone as far as banning Bitcoin but have issued warnings to the public and implemented regulatory measures to control its use. These measures often include anti-money laundering (AML) and know-your-customer (KYC) regulations that require cryptocurrency exchanges to verify the identities of their users and report suspicious activities. Central banks have also warned of the risks associated with investing in Bitcoin, including its volatility and the potential for financial loss.

Exploring Central Bank Digital Currencies (CBDCs):

• In response to the rise of Bitcoin, many central banks have begun exploring the development of their own digital currencies, known as Central Bank Digital Currencies (CBDCs). Unlike Bitcoin, CBDCs would be issued and controlled by central banks, allowing them to maintain control over the money supply and implement monetary policy in a digital environment. CBDCs are seen to modernize the financial system while preserving the central bank's authority. Countries like China, Sweden, and the European Union are already in advanced stages of developing and testing CBDCs.

Co-opting Blockchain Technology:

• Some central banks are also exploring ways to leverage the technology behind Bitcoin—blockchain—without adopting Bitcoin itself.

By using blockchain technology, central banks can create more efficient and secure financial systems while maintaining control over the currency. For example, some central banks are exploring the use of blockchain for interbank settlements, cross-border payments, and improving the security of financial transactions.

The Battle for Control: Central Banks vs. Bitcoin

The tension between central banks and Bitcoin is fundamentally a battle for control over the financial system. On one side are the central banks, which have long held the reins of monetary policy and financial regulation. On the other side is Bitcoin, a decentralized, borderless currency that operates outside the control of any central authority.

The Risks of Centralized Control:

- Proponents of Bitcoin argue that the centralized control exercised by central banks can lead to economic mismanagement, inflation, and financial crises. They point to events like the 2008 financial crisis as evidence of the dangers of entrusting monetary policy to a small group of decision-makers. Bitcoin, with its decentralized nature and fixed supply, is seen to protect against these risks by removing the power to print money or manipulate interest rates from the hands of central banks.

The Case for Stability and Regulation:

- On the other hand, central banks and their supporters argue that their control over monetary policy is necessary to maintain economic stability. They contend that the ability to adjust interest rates, control the money supply, and implement financial regulations is crucial for preventing inflation, managing economic growth, and responding to financial crises. In this view, Bitcoin's lack of central control and regulation makes it inherently unstable and risky, particularly as a global currency.

Potential for Coexistence:

- Despite the apparent conflict, there is also the possibility that central banks and Bitcoin could coexist in a more integrated financial system. Some central banks have expressed openness to the idea of allowing Bitcoin to function alongside national currencies if it is properly regulated. In this scenario, Bitcoin could serve as a store of value or a means of payment for certain types of transactions, while central banks retain control over the broader monetary system through CBDCs and traditional currencies.

The Future of Central Banks in a Bitcoin World

As Bitcoin continues to gain traction, central banks will need to adapt to a rapidly changing financial landscape. The rise of decentralized digital currencies presents both challenges and opportunities for these institutions.

Adapting to a Decentralized World:

- Central banks may need to rethink their approach to monetary policy and financial regulation in a world where decentralized currencies like Bitcoin exist. This could involve developing new tools and frameworks for managing the money supply, inflation, and financial stability in a digital economy. It may also require a shift in focus from controlling currency issuance to regulating the financial infrastructure that supports digital currencies.

Embracing Innovation:

- To remain relevant, central banks may need to embrace the technological innovations that have emerged from the cryptocurrency space. This includes not only the development of CBDCs but also the adoption of blockchain technology for other aspects of the financial system. By modernizing their operations and integrating digital currency solutions, central banks can maintain their role as key players in the global economy while adapting to new realities.

Navigating Regulatory Challenges:

- As more countries explore the adoption of Bitcoin and other cryptocurrencies, central banks will face increasing pressure to develop clear and consistent regulatory frameworks. This will require balancing the need to protect consumers and maintain financial stability with the desire to foster innovation and economic growth. The challenge will be to create regulations that allow for the coexistence of traditional financial systems and decentralized digital currencies without stifling innovation or undermining the authority of central banks.

The Ongoing Struggle for Financial Power

The rise of Bitcoin has sparked a fundamental debate about the future of money and the role of central banks in the global economy. As a decentralized digital currency, Bitcoin challenges the traditional financial system in ways that were unimaginable just a decade ago. Central banks, which have long held the reins of monetary policy and financial regulation, now find themselves in a battle for control over the future of money.

The outcome of this struggle is far from certain. Central banks have the tools and authority to influence the financial system in profound ways, but Bitcoin's growing popularity and adoption suggest that the demand for decentralized alternatives is strong. Whether central banks will adapt to this new reality, coexist with Bitcoin, or seek to suppress it remains to be seen.

As we move forward, the tension between centralized financial power and decentralized digital currencies will continue to shape the global economy. The decisions made by central banks, governments, and the Bitcoin community will determine the future of money and the balance of power in the financial system. One thing is clear: the world of finance is undergoing a transformation, and the stakes have never been higher.

8

The Invisible Hand: Central Bank Manipulation of Bitcoin Prices

As Bitcoin continues to establish itself as a significant player in the global financial system, questions have arisen about the role that central banks and other powerful financial institutions might play in influencing its price. The concept of the "invisible hand" is often used to describe the self-regulating nature of markets, but when it comes to Bitcoin, some believe that this hand is not as invisible as it seems. This chapter explores the theories and evidence suggesting that central banks or other influential entities may be manipulating Bitcoin prices to protect their interests, control market behavior, or maintain their hold on the financial system.

The Market Dynamics of Bitcoin

Before delving into the theories of price manipulation, it is important to understand the basic dynamics of the Bitcoin market. Bitcoin's price is determined by supply and demand, like any other asset. However, several unique factors influence these dynamics:

Limited Supply:

- Bitcoin's fixed supply of 21 million coins means that its price is highly sensitive to changes in demand. Unlike fiat currencies, which can be printed at will by central banks, the supply of Bitcoin is predetermined by its code. This scarcity is a key factor in its value proposition but also makes it more susceptible to price volatility.

Market Sentiment:

- The price of Bitcoin is heavily influenced by market sentiment, which can be driven by news, events, and public perception. Positive developments, such as the adoption of Bitcoin by major corporations, tend to drive prices up, while negative news, such as regulatory crackdowns, can lead to sharp declines.

Liquidity and Trading Volume:

- Bitcoin's market liquidity and trading volume also play a significant role in price determination. Although Bitcoin has grown significantly in market capitalization, it is still relatively insignificant compared to traditional financial markets. This means that large trades can have a disproportionate impact on the price, leading to volatility.

Theories of Central Bank Manipulation

Given the decentralized nature of Bitcoin, the idea that central banks or other powerful entities could manipulate its price might seem farfetched. However, several theories suggest that central banks have both the motive and the means to influence Bitcoin's market behavior.

Protecting National Currencies:

- One of the primary reasons central banks might seek to manipulate Bitcoin's price is to protect their national currencies. As Bitcoin gains popularity as an alternative store of value, it could undermine confidence in fiat currencies, particularly in countries with unstable or devalued currencies. By suppressing Bitcoin's price or creating uncertainty around it, central banks could discourage people from abandoning their national currencies in favor of Bitcoin.

Maintaining Control Over Monetary Policy:

- Central banks rely on their ability to control the money supply and influence interest rates to manage economic stability. If Bitcoin were to become widely adopted, it could weaken the effectiveness of these tools, as people might start using Bitcoin instead of traditional currencies. By manipulating Bitcoin's price, central banks could attempt to maintain control over the broader financial system and prevent Bitcoin from gaining too much influence.

Market Stability and Financial Stability:

- Some theorists suggest that central banks might manipulate Bitcoin's price to maintain overall market stability. Given Bitcoin's volatility, large price swings could have ripple effects on other financial markets, particularly as more institutional investors enter the space. By smoothing out these fluctuations, central banks could be attempting to protect the stability of the broader financial system.

Evidence of Potential Manipulation

While the theory of central bank manipulation is speculative, there are several instances and patterns in the Bitcoin market that have led some analysts to believe that manipulation could be at play.

The "Tether" Controversy:

- One of the most well-known allegations of Bitcoin price manipulation involves Tether, a stablecoin that is pegged to the US dollar. Some researchers have argued that Tether has been used to artificially inflate the price of Bitcoin by buying large amounts of Bitcoin with newly issued Tether during key market periods. This theory suggests that Tether's issuance is not fully backed by actual US dollars, meaning that the purchasing power is created out of thin air. If true, this could indicate a form of price manipulation, though whether central banks are directly involved remains unproven.

The 2017-2018 Bitcoin Bubble:

- The rapid rise and subsequent crash of Bitcoin's price in 2017-2018 has led to speculation that the market was being manipulated by large players, including central banks or financial institutions. During this period, Bitcoin's price rose from around $1,000 to $20,000, only to crash back down to below $4,000 in the following year. Some analysts believe that the timing of regulatory announcements, large selloffs, and negative media coverage may have been coordinated to trigger panic selling and depress the price.

Whales and Large Market Players:

- Another piece of circumstantial evidence comes from the behavior of "whales"—individuals or entities that hold large amounts of Bitcoin. Because the Bitcoin market is insignificant compared to traditional financial markets, whales have the power to move prices significantly by buying or selling large amounts of Bitcoin. Some believe that central banks or affiliated institutions could be acting like whales, using their market power to influence prices for strategic reasons.

The Mechanics of Manipulation

If central banks were indeed manipulating Bitcoin's price, how would they do it? Several mechanisms could potentially be used to exert influence over the market:

Futures Markets and Derivatives:

- One way to influence Bitcoin's price is using futures markets and derivatives. By taking large positions in Bitcoin futures, a central bank or financial institution could create pressure on the spot market price of Bitcoin. For example, by shorting Bitcoin futures (betting that the price will go down), they could incentivize selling in the spot market, driving the price down. This strategy could be used to create artificial price movements that do not reflect actual market demand.

Coordinated Media Campaigns:

- Another potential tool for manipulation is the media. As discussed in the previous chapter, media narratives can have a powerful impact on market sentiment. By strategically releasing negative news or regulatory announcements, central banks could create panic in the market, leading to price declines. Conversely, they could also use positive news to stabilize the market or encourage buying at key moments.

Liquidity Manipulation:

- Central banks could also influence Bitcoin's price by manipulating market liquidity. By either flooding the market with liquidity (through large sell orders) or withdrawing liquidity (by buying up Bitcoin), they could create artificial price movements. This would be particularly effective in a market as relatively illiquid as Bitcoin, where large trades can have outsized effects.

Regulatory Pressure and Legal Actions:

- Finally, central banks could use regulatory pressure and legal actions to influence the Bitcoin market. By enacting regulations that make it more difficult to buy, sell, or hold Bitcoin, they could suppress demand and lower the price. Similarly, by pursuing legal actions against major players in the Bitcoin market (such as exchanges), they could create uncertainty and drive down prices.

The Implications of Manipulation for Bitcoin's Future

If central bank manipulation of Bitcoin prices is indeed taking place, it raises significant questions about the future of Bitcoin and its role in the global financial system.

Challenges to Bitcoin's Decentralization:

- One of Bitcoin's core value propositions is its decentralization and resistance to control by any single entity. If central banks can manipulate its price, it could undermine this principle and call into question Bitcoin's ability to function as a truly decentralized currency. This could lead to a loss of confidence among users and investors, potentially limiting Bitcoin's adoption and growth.

Impact on Market Stability:

- Manipulation by central banks could also have a destabilizing effect on the Bitcoin market. If prices are artificially suppressed or inflated, it could create volatility that deters both retail and institutional investors. This could make Bitcoin less attractive as a store of value or medium of exchange, particularly if investors perceive it as being subject to manipulation.

The Potential for Pushback:

- On the other hand, evidence of manipulation could galvanize the Bitcoin community to push back against central banks and other powerful entities. This could lead to increased efforts to develop technologies and strategies that make Bitcoin more resistant to manipulation, such as decentralized exchanges, privacy enhancements, and more robust market infrastructure. It could also strengthen the narrative of Bitcoin as a tool for financial freedom and resistance to centralized control.

Long-Term Viability as a Global Currency:

- The question of central bank manipulation goes to the heart of Bitcoin's long-term viability as a global currency. If Bitcoin can withstand these pressures and continue to grow and evolve, it may prove itself as a resilient and enduring asset. However, if manipulation becomes a significant and persistent issue, it could limit Bitcoin's potential to achieve mainstream adoption and challenge the dominance of traditional financial systems.

The Unseen Forces Shaping Bitcoin's Market

The theory of central bank manipulation of Bitcoin prices adds a layer of complexity to the already intricate dynamics of the cryptocurrency market. While the evidence remains circumstantial, the possibility that powerful institutions are influencing Bitcoin's price cannot be entirely dismissed.

As Bitcoin continues to mature and integrate into the global financial system, the interplay between decentralized digital currencies and centralized financial power will be a key factor in shaping the future of money. Whether Bitcoin can maintain its independence and resist manipulation by central banks will be a critical test of its resilience and potential as a global currency.

In the meantime, the Bitcoin community and market participants must remain vigilant, aware of the potential for manipulation and prepared to adapt to the challenges that lie ahead. The invisible hand of the market may not always be as invisible as it seems, but the decentralized nature of Bitcoin gives it the tools and the potential to chart its own course in the face of these challenges.

9

The Institutionalization of Bitcoin

Bitcoin's journey from a niche digital currency to a significant asset class has been marked by increasing interest and participation from institutional investors. As traditional financial institutions, large corporations, and even governments begin to engage with Bitcoin, cryptocurrency is undergoing a process of institutionalization that could have profound implications for its future. This chapter explores the factors driving institutional adoption, the impact of this trend on the Bitcoin ecosystem, and the potential challenges and opportunities that arise as Bitcoin becomes more integrated into the mainstream financial system.

The Early Days: Bitcoin's Fringe Beginnings

In its early years, Bitcoin was ignored by institutional investors. It was seen as a fringe asset, primarily used by tech enthusiasts, libertarians, and those seeking to operate outside the traditional financial system. The volatile nature of Bitcoin's price, its association with illicit activities, and the lack of regulatory clarity made it an unappealing option for risk-averse institutional investors.

However, as Bitcoin matured and its potential as a store of value became more widely recognized, interest from institutional players

THE INSTITUTIONALIZATION OF BITCOIN

began to grow. The development of more robust market infrastructure, the introduction of regulated financial products, and the increasing acceptance of Bitcoin as a legitimate asset class have all contributed to the institutionalization of Bitcoin.

Factors Driving Institutional Adoption

Several key factors have driven the growing interest in Bitcoin among institutional investors:

Hedge Against Inflation and Economic Uncertainty:

- One of the primary motivations for institutional adoption of Bitcoin is its potential as a hedge against inflation and economic uncertainty. With central banks around the world engaging in unprecedented levels of monetary stimulus and quantitative easing, concerns about the devaluation of fiat currencies have increased. Bitcoin, with its fixed supply and decentralized nature, is seen by some as a form of "digital gold" that can preserve value in the face of inflationary pressures.

Diversification of Investment Portfolios:

- Institutional investors are increasingly looking to diversify their portfolios by including non-correlated assets that can provide returns independent of traditional markets. Bitcoin's unique properties, including its scarcity and decentralized nature, make it an attractive option for diversification. As a result, more hedge funds, asset managers, and pension funds are beginning to allocate a portion of their portfolios to Bitcoin.

Growing Market Maturity and Infrastructure:

- The maturation of the Bitcoin market has also played a crucial role in attracting institutional investors. The development of regulated exchanges, custodial services, and financial products like Bitcoin futures and exchange-traded funds (ETFs) has made it easier and safer for institutions to invest in Bitcoin. These developments have also helped to address concerns about security, liquidity, and regulatory compliance.

Corporate Adoption and Strategic Investments:

- In addition to financial institutions, large corporations have also begun to embrace Bitcoin as a strategic asset. Companies like Tesla, MicroStrategy, and Square have made headlines by adding Bitcoin to their balance sheets, viewing it as a long-term store of value. This corporate adoption has further legitimized Bitcoin and encouraged other companies to consider similar strategies.

Regulatory Clarity and Acceptance:

- The gradual clarification of regulatory frameworks for Bitcoin has also contributed to its institutionalization. As governments and regulatory bodies develop clearer guidelines for the use and trading of cryptocurrencies, institutional investors have gained greater confidence in entering the market. While regulatory approaches vary by country, the trend toward greater acceptance and regulation of Bitcoin is seen as a positive development for institutional adoption.

Impact of Institutional Adoption on the Bitcoin Ecosystem

The entry of institutional investors into the Bitcoin market has had a significant impact on the ecosystem, bringing both benefits and challenges.

Increased Market Stability and Liquidity:

- One of the most noticeable effects of institutional adoption has been the increase in market stability and liquidity. As more institutional capital flows into Bitcoin, the market has become less prone to extreme volatility, with deeper liquidity pools helping to absorb large trades without causing dramatic price swings. This increased stability is likely to make Bitcoin more attractive to a broader range of investors, including those who have been hesitant to enter the market due to concerns about volatility.

Price Appreciation and Market Capitalization:

- The influx of institutional capital has also contributed to significant price appreciation and an increase in Bitcoin's market capitalization. As demand for Bitcoin grows among institutional investors, the price tends to rise, attracting even more interest from both retail and institutional players. This positive feedback loop has been a key driver of Bitcoin's recent bull markets and has helped to solidify its position as a major asset class.

Development of Financial Products and Services:

- The institutionalization of Bitcoin has led to the development of a wide range of financial products and services designed to meet the needs of institutional investors. These include Bitcoin futures, options, ETFs, and custodial services, all of which make it easier for institutions to gain exposure to Bitcoin. The availability of these products has also made it possible for more conservative investors to participate in the Bitcoin market, further broadening its appeal.

Integration with Traditional Financial Systems:

- As Bitcoin becomes more institutionalized, it is increasingly being integrated with traditional financial systems. Banks, payment processors, and other financial institutions are beginning to offer Bitcoin-related services, such as custody, trading, and settlement. This integration is helping to bridge the gap between the traditional financial system and the world of digital assets, making it easier for institutions to incorporate Bitcoin into their existing operations.

Challenges of Institutionalization

While institutional adoption has brought many benefits to the Bitcoin ecosystem, it also presents several challenges that must be addressed as Bitcoin continues to evolve.

Centralization of Market Power:

- One of the potential downsides of institutionalization is the risk of centralization. As large financial institutions and corporations accumulate significant amounts of Bitcoin, there is a concern that they could gain disproportionate influence over the market. This could undermine the decentralized ethos of Bitcoin and lead to a concentration of power in the hands of a few large players. The presence of "whales" (entities that hold large amounts of Bitcoin) has already been a topic of concern, and increased institutional participation could exacerbate this issue.

Regulatory Scrutiny and Compliance:

- As more institutions enter the Bitcoin market, regulatory scrutiny is likely to increase. Governments and regulatory bodies may seek to impose stricter regulations on Bitcoin trading, custody, and other activities, potentially leading to a more regulated and less freewheeling market. While regulatory clarity can provide confidence to institutional investors, there is also a risk that overly burdensome regulations could stifle innovation and limit the growth of the Bitcoin ecosystem.

Potential for Market Manipulation:

- The involvement of large institutional players in the Bitcoin market raises concerns about the potential for market manipulation. Institutions with significant financial resources may be able to influence Bitcoin prices through large trades, short-selling strategies, or other means. This could create an uneven playing field, where smaller investors are at a disadvantage compared to larger, more powerful entities.

Impact on Bitcoin's Identity and Purpose:

- The institutionalization of Bitcoin also raises questions about its identity and purpose. Bitcoin was originally conceived as a decentralized, peer-to-peer digital currency that could operate outside the control of traditional financial institutions. As it becomes more integrated with the mainstream financial system, some fear that Bitcoin could lose its original ethos and become just another asset class, stripped of its revolutionary potential. The tension between Bitcoin's roots as a decentralized currency and its growing role as an institutional asset will be a key issue in the coming years.

Opportunities Arising from Institutionalization
Despite the challenges, the institutionalization of Bitcoin presents

several opportunities that could help to drive its adoption and success in the long term.

Broader Adoption and Mainstream Acceptance:

- Institutional adoption is likely to accelerate Bitcoin's mainstream acceptance. As more financial institutions and corporations embrace Bitcoin, it becomes easier for individuals and businesses to use and invest in it. This increased accessibility could lead to broader adoption, helping Bitcoin to achieve its potential as a global currency and store of value.

Development of New Use Cases:

- The involvement of institutional investors could also lead to the development of new use cases for Bitcoin. As institutions explore ways to integrate Bitcoin into their operations, new applications and innovations may emerge. For example, Bitcoin could be used as collateral for loans, integrated into payment systems, or utilized in cross-border trade. The creativity and resources of institutional players could unlock new possibilities for Bitcoin and expand its utility.

Increased Investment in Infrastructure and Technology:

- Institutional interest in Bitcoin is likely to drive increased investment in the infrastructure and technology that support the Bitcoin ecosystem. This could lead to improvements in areas such as scalability, security, and transaction speed, making Bitcoin more efficient and user-friendly. As the infrastructure around Bitcoin continues to develop, it will become easier for both individuals and institutions to participate in the market.

Enhanced Market Legitimacy and Stability:

- Finally, the institutionalization of Bitcoin is likely to enhance its legitimacy and stability as an asset class. As more institutions enter the market, Bitcoin will be seen as a more mature and credible investment, reducing the perception of it as a speculative or fringe asset. This increased legitimacy could attract a wider range of investors, including those who have been hesitant to invest in Bitcoin due to concerns about its volatility and regulatory status.

The Future of Institutional Bitcoin

As Bitcoin continues to evolve and integrate with the traditional financial system, the role of institutional investors will become even more prominent. The process of institutionalization is still in its early stages, and the coming years will be critical in determining how Bitcoin's relationship with the financial establishment develops.

Potential for a Hybrid Financial System:

- One potential outcome of Bitcoin's institutionalization is the development of a hybrid financial system, where traditional financial institutions and decentralized digital currencies coexist and complement each other. In this scenario, Bitcoin could serve as a store of value and medium of exchange alongside fiat currencies and other financial assets. Institutions could play a key role in bridging the gap between these two worlds, helping to create a more integrated and flexible financial system.

Ongoing Tension Between Decentralization and Centralization:

- However, the tension between Bitcoin's decentralized origins and its growing institutionalization is likely to persist. As institutions gain more influence in the Bitcoin market, there will be ongoing debates about how to preserve the principles of decentralization and autonomy that are central to Bitcoin's identity. Balancing these competing forces will be a key challenge for the Bitcoin community and the broader financial industry.

The Role of Regulation in Shaping the Future:

- Regulation will also play a crucial role in shaping the future of institutional Bitcoin. Governments and regulatory bodies will need to strike a balance between protecting investors, ensuring market integrity, and fostering innovation. The regulatory frameworks that emerge will have a significant impact on how Bitcoin is used, traded, and integrated into the global financial system.

A New Era for Bitcoin

The institutionalization of Bitcoin marks a new era in cryptocurrency's journey from a niche digital experiment to a mainstream financial asset. As more financial institutions, corporations, and governments engage with Bitcoin, it is becoming increasingly clear that Bitcoin is here to stay.

While the process of institutionalization brings challenges and raises important questions about Bitcoin's identity and future, it also presents significant opportunities for broader adoption, innovation, and integration into the global financial system. As Bitcoin continues to evolve, the relationship between decentralized digital currencies and the traditional financial establishment will be a defining factor in the future of money.

Whether Bitcoin remains true to its decentralized roots or becomes more intertwined with the institutions it was designed to circumvent, its impact on the financial world is undeniable. The ongoing institutionalization of Bitcoin is a testament to its resilience, adaptability, and potential to shape the future of finance in profound ways.

10

Bitcoin's Future in a New World Financial System

As Bitcoin continues to establish itself as a key player in the global financial landscape, the question of its future becomes increasingly relevant. Will Bitcoin become the cornerstone of a new world financial system, or will it remain a niche asset, coexisting with traditional currencies? This chapter explores the various scenarios that could unfold as Bitcoin's role in the global economy evolves, considering the potential paths for its integration, challenges it may face, and the broader implications for the world's financial system.

Scenario 1: Bitcoin as a Parallel Currency

One of the most plausible scenarios is that Bitcoin will function as a parallel currency alongside traditional fiat currencies. In this role, Bitcoin would not replace national currencies but would exist alongside them, offering an alternative form of money that people and businesses can choose to use depending on their needs and preferences.

Advantages of Bitcoin as a Parallel Currency:

- **Financial Sovereignty:** Bitcoin's decentralized nature allows individuals to maintain greater control over their finances, independent of government policies or central bank decisions. This financial sovereignty is particularly appealing in countries with unstable economies or authoritarian regimes.

- **Cross-Border Transactions:** Bitcoin's ability to facilitate low-cost, fast cross-border transactions makes it an attractive option for international trade and remittances. By reducing reliance on traditional banking systems, Bitcoin can provide a more efficient and inclusive global financial system.

- **Inflation Hedge:** In countries experiencing high inflation or currency devaluation, Bitcoin could serve as a hedge against the loss of purchasing power. As a parallel currency, it would allow people to protect their wealth while still using their local currency for day-to-day transactions.

Challenges of Bitcoin as a Parallel Currency:

- **Regulatory Acceptance:** For Bitcoin to function effectively as a parallel currency, governments and regulators would need to establish clear and supportive regulatory frameworks. However, the decentralized and borderless nature of Bitcoin may pose challenges to its regulation, particularly in countries that view it as a threat to their monetary sovereignty.

- **Adoption and Integration:** Widespread adoption of Bitcoin as a parallel currency would require significant infrastructure development, including payment systems, merchant acceptance, and user education. While progress is being made, achieving the level of adoption necessary for Bitcoin to function as a parallel currency will take time and effort.

- **Volatility:** Bitcoin's price volatility remains a significant challenge to its use as a currency. For Bitcoin to be widely adopted as a medium of exchange, its value would need to stabilize, reducing the risks associated with using it for everyday transactions.

Scenario 2: Bitcoin as a Global Reserve Currency

Another potential scenario is that Bitcoin could evolve into a global reserve currency, like the role gold has played historically. In this scenario, central banks and governments would hold Bitcoin as part of their foreign exchange reserves, using it to back their national currencies and stabilize their economies.

Advantages of Bitcoin as a Global Reserve Currency:

- **Decentralization and Trust:** As a decentralized currency, Bitcoin is not subject to the control of any single government or central bank. This makes it an attractive option for countries looking to diversify their reserves and reduce their reliance on traditional reserve currencies like the US dollar.
- **Fixed Supply:** Bitcoin's fixed supply of 21 million coins provides a level of predictability and stability that is appealing in the context of a global reserve currency. Unlike fiat currencies, which can be inflated at the discretion of central banks, Bitcoin's supply is governed by its code, reducing the risk of devaluation.
- **Global Acceptance:** As Bitcoin's adoption grows, it could become increasingly accepted as a universal form of money, transcending national borders, and serving as a common standard for international trade and finance.

Challenges of Bitcoin as a Global Reserve Currency:

- **Resistance from Central Banks:** Central banks may be reluctant to adopt Bitcoin as a reserve currency, as it would limit their ability to implement monetary policy and control their national economies. The transition to a Bitcoin-based reserve system would require significant changes to the existing financial infrastructure and could face resistance from powerful institutions.

- **Technological and Security Concerns:** The security and scalability of the Bitcoin network would need to be continually improved to support its role as a global reserve currency. Any vulnerabilities or weaknesses in the system could undermine confidence in Bitcoin and limit its acceptance as a reserve asset.

- **Market Volatility:** For Bitcoin to function as a global reserve currency, its price volatility would need to be addressed. Central banks are likely to be cautious about holding an asset that can experience significant price fluctuations, as this could introduce instability into their reserves.

Scenario 3: Bitcoin as the Dominant Global Currency

A more ambitious scenario is that Bitcoin could become the dominant global currency, replacing, or significantly displacing traditional fiat currencies. In this scenario, Bitcoin would be used for many transactions worldwide, serving as the primary medium of exchange, store of value, and unit of account.

Advantages of Bitcoin as the Dominant Global Currency:

- **Uniformity and Simplicity:** A single global currency like Bitcoin would eliminate the need for currency exchange, simplifying international trade and reducing transaction costs. This could lead to greater economic efficiency and integration, particularly in the context of a globalized economy.

- **Financial Inclusion:** Bitcoin's decentralized nature and low barriers to entry could promote greater financial inclusion, particularly in developing countries where access to traditional banking services is limited. By providing a universal and accessible form of money, Bitcoin could help bridge the gap between the developed and developing worlds.

- **Resilience to Political and Economic Shocks:** As a global currency, Bitcoin would be less susceptible to the political and economic decisions of individual governments. This could reduce the impact of currency crises, hyperinflation, and other forms of economic instability.

Challenges of Bitcoin as the Dominant Global Currency:

- **Adoption and Transition:** Transitioning to a Bitcoin-based global currency system would require widespread adoption and significant changes to existing financial infrastructure. Governments, businesses, and individuals would need to be willing to embrace Bitcoin as their primary form of money, which could be a slow and challenging process.
- **Regulatory and Political Resistance:** The adoption of Bitcoin as the dominant global currency would face significant resistance from governments and central banks, who would lose control over their monetary policy and economic sovereignty. This resistance could manifest in the form of restrictive regulations, legal challenges, and even attempts to suppress or ban Bitcoin.
- **Scalability and Environmental Impact:** Bitcoin's current scalability limitations and the environmental impact of its proof-of-work consensus mechanism are significant obstacles to its widespread adoption as a global currency. Addressing these challenges would require technological advancements and potentially a shift to more sustainable consensus mechanisms.

Scenario 4: Bitcoin as a Niche Asset

In this scenario, Bitcoin remains a niche asset, primarily used as a store of value and a speculative investment rather than a mainstream currency. While Bitcoin continues to attract attention and investment, it has not achieved widespread adoption as a medium of exchange or global currency.

Advantages of Bitcoin as a Niche Asset:

- **Preservation of Value:** Bitcoin's role as a store of value, akin to digital gold, would be preserved in this scenario. Investors would continue to use Bitcoin as a hedge against inflation and economic uncertainty, benefiting from its fixed supply and decentralized nature.
- **Reduced Regulatory Pressure:** If Bitcoin remains a niche asset, it may face less regulatory scrutiny and pressure compared to if it were to become a dominant global currency. This could allow the Bitcoin community to continue innovating and developing new use cases without the constraints of heavy-handed regulation.
- **Focus on Core Strengths:** By remaining a niche asset, Bitcoin can focus on its core strengths—decentralization, security, and scarcity—without being stretched thin by the demands of functioning as a global currency.

Challenges of Bitcoin as a Niche Asset:

- **Limited Adoption and Use Cases:** If Bitcoin remains a niche asset, its adoption and use cases will be limited to a small segment of the population. This could limit its impact on the broader financial system and reduce its potential to drive meaningful change in the way money is used and understood.
- **Vulnerability to Competition:** As a niche asset, Bitcoin may face competition from other cryptocurrencies or digital assets that offer more advanced features, better scalability, or more regulatory compliance. Without broader adoption, Bitcoin could

be overshadowed by new innovations in the digital currency space.

- **Perception of Speculation:** If Bitcoin remains primarily a speculative asset, it may struggle to shake the perception that it is a risky and volatile investment. This could limit its appeal to more conservative investors and hinder its long-term growth potential.

Implications for the Global Financial System

The future of Bitcoin, whether as a parallel currency, global reserve, dominant currency, or niche asset, will have significant implications for the global financial system.

Decentralization vs. Centralization:

- The rise of Bitcoin has sparked a broader debate about the balance between decentralization and centralization in the global financial system. Bitcoin's success could lead to a shift towards more decentralized and distributed financial models, challenging the dominance of central banks and large financial institutions. However, this shift will face resistance from established powers that have a personal stake in maintaining centralized control.

Monetary Policy and Economic Stability:

- The integration of Bitcoin into the global financial system could fundamentally alter the way monetary policy is conducted. Central banks may need to develop new tools and strategies to manage economies in a world where Bitcoin plays a significant role. The impact on economic stability will depend on how well Bitcoin's volatility can be managed and how effectively it can be integrated into existing monetary frameworks.

Financial Inclusion and Global Inequality:

- Bitcoin's potential to promote financial inclusion and reduce global inequality is one of its most promising features. By providing access to financial services for unbanked and underbanked populations, Bitcoin could help level the playing field and empower individuals in developing countries. However, realizing this potential will require concerted efforts to build the necessary infrastructure and educate users.

- **Innovation and Competition:**
- The rise of Bitcoin is likely to drive further innovation and competition in the digital currency space. As modern technologies and cryptocurrencies emerge, they will challenge Bitcoin's dominance and push the boundaries of what is possible in the world of digital finance. This competition will be beneficial for consumers, as it will lead to better products, services, and user experiences.

Charting Bitcoin's Path Forward

The future of Bitcoin is still unfolding, and its ultimate role in the global financial system remains uncertain. Whether Bitcoin becomes a parallel currency, a global reserve, a dominant currency, or a niche asset will depend on a complex interplay of factors, including technological advancements, regulatory developments, market dynamics, and public perception.

As Bitcoin continues to evolve, it will be essential for all stakeholders—governments, financial institutions, businesses, and individuals—to engage thoughtfully and proactively with this emerging asset class. The decisions made today will shape the future of money and finance for generations to come.

Bitcoin's journey is far from over, and its potential to reshape the global financial system is immense. Whether it achieves this potential or not, Bitcoin has already left an indelible mark on the world of finance, challenging long-held assumptions, and opening the door to new possibilities. As we move forward, the key question will be how we harness the power of Bitcoin to create a more inclusive, equitable, and resilient financial system for all.

11

The Power Struggle: Central Banks vs. Bitcoin

The rise of Bitcoin has brought to the forefront a fundamental power struggle between decentralized digital currencies and the traditional financial institutions that have long controlled the global economy. Central banks, which have been the bedrock of monetary policy and financial stability for centuries, now face a significant challenge from Bitcoin—a currency that operates outside their control. This chapter explores the ongoing battle between central banks and Bitcoin, examining the strategies employed by both sides, the potential outcomes of this conflict, and what it means for the future of money.

The Authority of Central Banks

Central banks play a crucial role in managing national economies and maintaining financial stability. Their primary functions include controlling the money supply, setting interest rates, regulating financial institutions, and acting as lenders of last resort during economic crises. Through these mechanisms, central banks influence inflation, employment, and overall economic growth.

Monetary Policy and Control:

- Central banks exert control over monetary policy by adjusting interest rates and conducting open market operations, such as buying and selling government bonds. These actions influence the cost of borrowing and the availability of credit, which in turn affects economic activity and inflation. This ability to manage the economy through monetary policy is a core function of central banks and is critical to their power.

Currency Issuance and Sovereignty:

- Central banks have the exclusive authority to issue national currencies, which are considered legal tender within their respective countries. This monopoly on currency issuance allows central banks to control the money supply and manage inflation. It also reinforces the concept of national sovereignty, as each country's currency is tied to its government and economy.

Regulation and Stability:

- Central banks are also responsible for regulating the financial system to ensure its stability. This includes overseeing commercial banks, implementing capital requirements, and enforcing anti-money laundering (AML) and know-your-customer (KYC) regulations. By maintaining the stability of the financial system, central banks aim to prevent financial crises and protect consumers.

The Challenge of Bitcoin

Bitcoin, as a decentralized digital currency, presents a direct challenge to the authority of central banks. Unlike fiat currencies, Bitcoin is not issued or controlled by any central authority. Instead, it operates on a peer-to-peer network where transactions are verified by a distributed network of nodes and recorded on a public ledger known as the blockchain. This decentralized nature is at the heart of Bitcoin's appeal— and its threat to central banks.

Decentralization and Financial Sovereignty:

- Bitcoin's decentralization means that no single entity can control its supply or influence its value. This is in stark contrast to fiat currencies, which central banks can manipulate through monetary policy. For proponents of Bitcoin, this decentralization represents financial sovereignty—an escape from the control of central banks and governments. However, for central banks, it represents a loss of power and influence over the economy.

Fixed Supply and Inflation Resistance:

- Bitcoin's fixed supply of 21 million coins is another feature that challenges the traditional role of central banks. Unlike fiat currencies, which can be printed in unlimited quantities, Bitcoin's supply is capped, making it inherently deflationary. This resistance to inflation is one of the reasons Bitcoin has been dubbed "digital gold." However, it also limits the ability of central banks to manage inflation through traditional monetary policy tools.

Alternative Financial Systems:

- Bitcoin's rise has also given birth to an alternative financial ecosystem, including decentralized finance (DeFi) platforms, cryptocurrency exchanges, and blockchain-based payment systems. These alternatives operate outside the traditional banking system, reducing the reliance on central banks and commercial banks for financial services. As this ecosystem grows, it could further erode the influence of central banks over the global economy.

Central Bank Strategies to Counter Bitcoin

Recognizing the threat posed by Bitcoin, central banks around the world have adopted various strategies to counter its rise. These strategies range from outright opposition to attempts to co-opt the technology behind Bitcoin.

Regulatory Crackdowns:

- One of the most common strategies employed by central banks is the implementation of strict regulations aimed at curbing the use of Bitcoin and other cryptocurrencies. These regulations often target cryptocurrency exchanges, requiring them to comply with AML and KYC regulations. In some cases, governments have gone further, banning the use of cryptocurrencies altogether. China, for example, has implemented a series of crackdowns on Bitcoin mining and trading, effectively driving these activities underground or out of the country.

Development of Central Bank Digital Currencies (CBDCs):

- In response to the rise of Bitcoin, many central banks have begun exploring the development of their own digital currencies, known as Central Bank Digital Currencies (CBDCs). CBDCs are digital versions of a country's fiat currency, issued and controlled by the central bank. Unlike Bitcoin, which operates on a decentralized network, CBDCs would be centralized and subject to the same monetary policies as traditional currencies. The development of CBDCs is seen as a way for central banks to modernize their financial systems while maintaining control over the money supply.

Public Discourse and Education:

- Central banks have also engaged in public discourse and educational efforts to warn the public about the risks associated with Bitcoin. These efforts often focus on Bitcoin's volatility, its use in illegal activities, and the lack of consumer protections. By highlighting these risks, central banks aim to discourage people from using or investing in Bitcoin and to reinforce trust in traditional financial systems.

Monetary Policy Adjustments:

- Some central banks have adjusted their monetary policies in response to the rise of Bitcoin and other cryptocurrencies. For example, they may tighten or loosen monetary policy to influence the attractiveness of fiat currencies relative to Bitcoin. By maintaining low inflation and stable economic conditions, central banks can reduce the appeal of Bitcoin as a hedge against economic instability.

Bitcoin's Counterstrategies

While central banks have taken steps to counter Bitcoin, the Bitcoin community has also developed strategies to resist these efforts and promote the adoption of decentralized digital currencies.

Advancing Technology and Security:

- One of the primary strategies employed by the Bitcoin community is the continuous improvement of the technology that underpins Bitcoin. This includes efforts to enhance the scalability, security, and privacy of the Bitcoin network. The development of the Lightning Network, for example, aims to address Bitcoin's scalability issues by enabling faster and cheaper transactions. Similarly, ongoing research into privacy features seeks to make Bitcoin transactions more anonymous, reducing the ability of governments and central banks to track and control its use.

Promoting Decentralized Finance (DeFi):

- The growth of the DeFi ecosystem represents another strategy for advancing the adoption of decentralized digital currencies. DeFi platforms offer financial services such as lending, borrowing, and trading without the need for traditional intermediaries like banks. By providing alternatives to the traditional financial system, DeFi strengthens the appeal of Bitcoin and other cryptocurrencies, challenging the dominance of central banks.

Grassroots Advocacy and Education:

- The Bitcoin community has also engaged in grassroots advocacy and education efforts to promote the benefits of decentralized digital currencies. This includes creating educational content, hosting conferences, and engaging with policymakers to advocate for more favorable regulatory environments. By building a strong and informed community, Bitcoin advocates aim to increase adoption and resistance to central bank efforts to suppress or control Bitcoin.

Building Resilience Against Censorship:

- To counter the risk of censorship by governments and central banks, the Bitcoin community has focused on building resilience into the network. This includes the development of decentralized exchanges (DEXs) that operate without central authority and are more difficult to shut down. Additionally, efforts to improve the privacy and anonymity of Bitcoin transactions help protect users from government surveillance and censorship.

Potential Outcomes of the Power Struggle

The ongoing power struggle between central banks and Bitcoin could lead to several outcomes, each with significant implications for the future of money and the global financial system.

Coexistence and Integration:

- One potential outcome is that Bitcoin and central banks will find a way to coexist, with Bitcoin functioning as a complementary asset alongside traditional fiat currencies. In this scenario, Bitcoin could serve as a store of value or a means of international trade, while central banks continue to manage national economies using fiat currencies and CBDCs. This coexistence would require mutual recognition and cooperation between the two systems, as well as regulatory frameworks that allow for the integration of Bitcoin into the broader financial system.

Suppression of Bitcoin:

- Another outcome is that central banks and governments succeed in suppressing the use of Bitcoin, either through stringent regulations, legal restrictions, or technological measures. This could limit Bitcoin's adoption and push it to the margins of the financial system. While it is unlikely that Bitcoin could be completely eradicated due to its decentralized nature, its role in the global economy could be significantly diminished if central banks take aggressive action against it.

Bitcoin's Ascendancy:

- Conversely, Bitcoin could emerge victorious in this power struggle, gaining widespread adoption and challenging the dominance of fiat currencies and central banks. In this scenario, Bitcoin could become a global standard for value transfer and storage, reducing the influence of central banks over the global economy. This outcome would be driven by a combination of technological advancements, grassroots support, and a growing distrust of traditional financial institutions.

Fragmentation of the Financial System:

- A fourth possibility is that the power struggle between Bitcoin and central banks leads to a more fragmented global financial system. In this scenario, different regions or countries may adopt varying approaches to Bitcoin, with some embracing it and others rejecting it. This could result in a patchwork of financial systems, where Bitcoin coexists with fiat currencies, CBDCs, and other digital assets in a complex and diverse global economy.

The Broader Implications for Money and Power

The outcome of the power struggle between central banks and Bitcoin will have far-reaching implications for the future of money, power, and financial sovereignty.

Redefining Money:

- Bitcoin challenges traditional notions of money by introducing a decentralized, digital form of currency that operates outside the control of governments and central banks. As Bitcoin and other cryptocurrencies gain traction, the very definition of money may evolve, leading to new forms of value exchange that are more inclusive, transparent, and resistant to censorship.

Shifting Power Dynamics:

- The rise of Bitcoin has the potential to shift power dynamics within the global financial system. Central banks, which have long held a monopoly on currency issuance and monetary policy, may see their influence wane as decentralized digital currencies gain popularity. This could lead to a redistribution of financial power, with individuals and communities gaining greater control over their money and economic decisions.

Empowering Individuals:

- One of the most profound implications of Bitcoin is its potential to empower individuals by giving them greater control over their finances. By removing the need for intermediaries and providing access to a global, decentralized financial system, Bitcoin can help people protect their wealth, resist economic oppression, and participate in the global economy on their own terms.

The Battle for the Future of Money

The power struggle between central banks and Bitcoin is a defining conflict of the 21st century, with profound implications for the future of money and the global financial system. As Bitcoin continues to challenge the traditional financial order, central banks are forced to adapt, innovate, and defend their authority.

The outcome of this struggle is far from certain, and it will be shaped by a combination of technological advancements, regulatory decisions, and shifts in public perception. Whether Bitcoin emerges as a dominant force in the global economy or remains a fringe asset, its impact on the world of finance is undeniable.

As we move forward, the key question will be how to balance the benefits of decentralization and financial sovereignty with the need for stability, regulation, and trust in the financial system. The choices we make today will determine the future of money and the role that Bitcoin will play in shaping it.

12

The Long-Term Viability of Bitcoin as a World Currency

As Bitcoin continues to evolve and gain traction in the global financial system, the question of its long-term viability as a world currency becomes increasingly pertinent. Can Bitcoin sustain its momentum and fulfill its potential as a decentralized global currency, or will it face insurmountable challenges that limit its role in the financial landscape? This chapter explores the key factors that will determine Bitcoin's future, including technological developments, regulatory challenges, market dynamics, and the broader economic environment.

Technological Advancements: Scaling and Security

One of the most critical factors influencing Bitcoin's long-term viability is its technological foundation. As Bitcoin's adoption grows, so too does the need for advancements in its scalability, security, and overall functionality.

Scalability Solutions:

- Bitcoin's scalability has been a persistent challenge, particularly as the network has grown. The Bitcoin blockchain can only process a limited number of transactions per second, leading to congestion and higher transaction fees during periods of high demand. To address this issue, several solutions have been proposed and implemented, including the Lightning Network, which enables faster and cheaper transactions by processing them off-chain. Continued development and widespread adoption of such scaling solutions will be crucial for Bitcoin to function effectively as a global currency.

Security Enhancements:

- Security is paramount for any currency, and Bitcoin's decentralized nature presents unique challenges and opportunities. While Bitcoin's blockchain is highly secure due to its proof-of-work consensus mechanism, it is not immune to threats. Potential vulnerabilities include 51% attacks, where a malicious entity gains control of most of the network's hashing power, and advances in quantum computing that could break current cryptographic standards. Ongoing research and development in cryptographic techniques, network architecture, and consensus mechanisms will be essential to maintaining Bitcoin's security and trustworthiness.

Privacy and Fungibility:

- Privacy and fungibility—where each unit of currency is indistinguishable from another—are important characteristics of a viable global currency. While Bitcoin transactions are transparent and traceable on the blockchain, there is a growing demand for enhanced privacy features. Technologies such as Schnorr signatures, Taproot, and CoinJoin are being developed to improve privacy and fungibility on the Bitcoin network. These advancements could help Bitcoin meet the privacy expectations of users and compete with

THE LONG-TERM VIABILITY OF BITCOIN AS A WORLD CURRENCY

other cryptocurrencies that offer more robust privacy features.

Regulatory Challenges and Opportunities

The regulatory environment will play a significant role in shaping Bitcoin's future as a world currency. Governments and regulatory bodies around the world have taken varying approaches to Bitcoin, ranging from outright bans to enthusiastic support. The development of clear and consistent regulatory frameworks will be crucial for Bitcoin's long-term success.

- **Global Regulatory Coordination:**
- One of the key challenges for Bitcoin is the lack of global regulatory coordination. Different countries have adopted different stances on Bitcoin, leading to a fragmented regulatory landscape. For Bitcoin to achieve its potential as a global currency, there will need to be greater harmonization of regulations across districts. This could involve the establishment of international standards for cryptocurrency regulation, ensuring that Bitcoin can be used and traded freely across borders without facing conflicting legal requirements.
- **Balancing Innovation and Protection:**
- Regulators face the challenging task of balancing the need to protect consumers and maintain financial stability with the desire to foster innovation in the cryptocurrency space. Overly restrictive regulations could stifle the growth of Bitcoin and limit its adoption, while a lack of regulation could expose users to risks such as fraud, market manipulation, and cyberattacks. The development of a regulatory environment that supports innovation while ensuring the safety and security of the financial system will be key to Bitcoin's long-term viability.
- **Regulatory Acceptance and Integration:**

- As Bitcoin becomes more integrated into the global financial system, regulatory acceptance will be crucial. Governments and central banks may need to adapt their monetary policies and financial regulations to accommodate the unique characteristics of Bitcoin. This could involve the development of new regulatory frameworks that recognize Bitcoin as a legitimate form of money, as well as the integration of Bitcoin into existing financial systems, such as payment networks and banking infrastructure.

Market Dynamics and Adoption

The dynamics of the Bitcoin market, including its adoption by individuals, businesses, and institutions, will also play a critical role in determining its long-term viability as a world currency.

- **Widespread Adoption:**
- For Bitcoin to function effectively as a global currency, it must achieve widespread adoption across different sectors of the economy. This includes not only individual users but also businesses, financial institutions, and governments. The more widely Bitcoin is accepted and used, the more likely it is to become a stable and reliable medium of exchange. Efforts to promote education, increase accessibility, and build user-friendly infrastructure will be key to driving broader adoption.
- **Institutional Involvement:**
- The involvement of institutional investors and large corporations has already had a significant impact on Bitcoin's market dynamics. As more institutions embrace Bitcoin as a strategic asset, it will help to legitimize and stabilize the market, attracting more participants. However, the increasing influence of institutional players also raises concerns about centralization and market manipulation. Striking a balance between institutional involvement and the preservation

of Bitcoin's decentralized ethos will be crucial for its long-term success.

- **Volatility and Market Maturity:**
- Bitcoin's price volatility has been one of the primary obstacles to its adoption as a global currency. For Bitcoin to be widely used as a medium of exchange, its price must stabilize to a level where businesses and individuals can use it with confidence. Market maturity, including the development of more sophisticated financial products and services, could help reduce volatility over time. Additionally, as the market grows and liquidity increases, Bitcoin's price may become less susceptible to large swings caused by individual trades or market events.

Economic and Environmental Considerations

The broader economic and environmental context will also influence Bitcoin's long-term viability as a world currency.

- **Global Economic Conditions:**
- The global economic environment will have a significant impact on Bitcoin's future. Economic instability, inflation, and currency devaluation could drive demand for Bitcoin as a store of value and alternative currency. Conversely, stable economic conditions and effective monetary policies could reduce the need for Bitcoin as a hedge against economic uncertainty. Understanding the interplay between global economic trends and Bitcoin's adoption will be critical for predicting its long-term viability.
- **Environmental Sustainability:**
- Bitcoin's environmental impact has become an increasingly important consideration, particularly as concerns about climate change and sustainability grow. The energy-intensive nature of Bitcoin mining, driven by its proof-of-work consensus mechanism, has led

to criticism and calls for more sustainable alternatives. Efforts to reduce Bitcoin's carbon footprint, such as the use of renewable energy sources and the development of more energy-efficient mining technologies, will be crucial for ensuring its long-term viability. Additionally, ongoing debates about transitioning to alternative consensus mechanisms, such as proof-of-stake, could shape the future of Bitcoin's environmental impact.

The Role of Competing Cryptocurrencies

Bitcoin is not the only cryptocurrency vying for a role in the global financial system. The emergence of competing cryptocurrencies, each with their own unique features and use cases, presents both challenges and opportunities for Bitcoin.

- **Competition and Innovation:**
- The presence of competing cryptocurrencies, such as Ethereum, Litecoin, and newer entrants like Solana and Cardano, fosters innovation in the broader cryptocurrency ecosystem. These cryptocurrencies offer distinctive features, such as smart contracts, faster transaction times, and lower fees, which may appeal to different user segments. While this competition could challenge Bitcoin's dominance, it also drives technological advancements that could benefit the entire ecosystem.
- **Bitcoin's Unique Value Proposition:**
- Despite the rise of competing cryptocurrencies, Bitcoin's unique value proposition as the first and most widely recognized cryptocurrency gives it a significant advantage. Bitcoin's fixed supply, decentralized nature, and strong network effects make it a powerful store of value and a reliable form of digital money. If Bitcoin continues to innovate and adapt, it is likely to maintain its position as the leading cryptocurrency, even in the face of competition.

Potential Scenarios for Bitcoin's Future

As Bitcoin navigates the various challenges and opportunities outlined in this chapter, several potential scenarios could emerge for its long-term role in the global financial system:

- **Bitcoin as a Global Reserve Asset:**
- In this scenario, Bitcoin becomes a widely accepted global reserve asset, akin to digital gold. Central banks, institutions, and individuals hold Bitcoin as a store of value and a hedge against economic instability. While Bitcoin may not replace traditional currencies, it serves as a trusted and universally recognized form of wealth preservation.
- **Bitcoin as a Niche Store of Value:**
- Bitcoin remains a niche store of value, primarily used by investors and those seeking to preserve wealth outside of traditional financial systems. In this scenario, Bitcoin does not achieve widespread adoption as a medium of exchange but continues to be valued for its scarcity, security, and decentralization.
- **Bitcoin as a Dominant Global Currency:**
- Bitcoin evolves into a dominant global currency, used for everyday transactions, international trade, and as a unit of account. In this scenario, Bitcoin's technological advancements, regulatory acceptance, and market dynamics align to make it a widely used and stable global currency.
- **Bitcoin as a Complementary Currency:**
- Bitcoin functions as a complementary currency alongside traditional fiat currencies and other digital assets. It is used for specific purposes, such as cross-border transactions, online commerce, or as a store of value, while traditional currencies continue to dominate most economic activities.

Bitcoin's Journey Ahead

The long-term viability of Bitcoin as a world currency will depend on a complex interplay of technological, regulatory, market, and environmental factors. As Bitcoin continues to evolve, it will face both opportunities and challenges that will shape its role in the global financial system.

Bitcoin's journey from a niche digital experiment to a potential global currency is far from over. The decisions made by developers, regulators, investors, and the broader community will determine whether Bitcoin can fulfill its promise as a decentralized, borderless form of money or whether it will remain a niche asset in the digital economy.

One thing is certain: Bitcoin has already made a profound impact on the world of finance, challenging traditional notions of money, power, and financial sovereignty. As we look to the future, the key question will be how Bitcoin can continue to innovate, adapt, and thrive in an ever-changing global landscape. Whether Bitcoin becomes a world currency or takes on another role in the financial system, its legacy as a transformative force in the digital age is secure.

13

Conclusion

The Legacy and Future of Bitcoin

Bitcoin's journey from its inception in 2009 to its status as a global financial phenomenon has been nothing short of remarkable. What began as a niche digital currency envisioned by an anonymous creator has grown into a powerful and disruptive force that challenges traditional financial systems, inspires innovation, and raises profound questions about the future of money and power.

Throughout this book, we have explored the many facets of Bitcoin's evolution: its mysterious origins, the media's role in shaping its image, the potential for manipulation by powerful institutions, and the ongoing struggle between Bitcoin and central banks. We have examined the institutionalization of Bitcoin, the technological advancements necessary for its success, and the various scenarios that could unfold as it continues to integrate into the global financial system.

Bitcoin's Impact on the World

Bitcoin has already left an indelible mark on the world of finance. It has introduced the concept of decentralized digital currency, sparking a wave of innovation that has given rise to thousands of cryptocurrencies and blockchain-based projects. It has challenged the authority of central banks and governments, offering individuals an alternative form of money that operates outside traditional control. Bitcoin has also demonstrated the power of technology to create new forms of value, redefine economic relationships, and empower people around the world.

As a store of value, Bitcoin has been compared to digital gold, offering a hedge against inflation and economic instability. As a medium of exchange, it has facilitated cross-border transactions, enabled financial inclusion, and provided a lifeline for those in countries with unstable currencies. And as a symbol, Bitcoin represents the ideals of financial sovereignty, decentralization, and resistance to censorship.

The Challenges Ahead

Despite its achievements, Bitcoin faces significant challenges as it continues to evolve. Scalability, security, and environmental sustainability are ongoing concerns that must be addressed for Bitcoin to achieve its full potential. The regulatory landscape remains uncertain, with governments and central banks grappling with how to integrate or control a currency that defies traditional financial norms. Market volatility and the presence of competing cryptocurrencies add further complexity to Bitcoin's future.

The power struggle between Bitcoin and central banks is particularly critical. As governments and financial institutions seek to protect their authority and control, they may implement regulations or develop alternatives like Central Bank Digital Currencies (CBDCs) that challenge Bitcoin's role in the financial system. How Bitcoin navigates these challenges will determine whether it can become a truly global currency or remain a niche asset.

The Future of Bitcoin

Looking ahead, Bitcoin's future is full of possibilities. It could become a dominant global currency, a universal store of value, or a complementary asset within a diversified financial system. The path it takes will depend on a range of factors, including technological advancements, regulatory developments, market dynamics, and broader economic trends.

Whatever the future holds, Bitcoin's influence on the financial world is undeniable. It has sparked a revolution in how we think about money, ownership, and value. It has opened the door to new forms of financial innovation and challenged the status quo in ways that were unimaginable just a decade ago.

A New Financial Paradigm

Bitcoin represents more than just a digital currency; it symbolizes a new financial paradigm—one that prioritizes decentralization, transparency, and individual empowerment. As we continue to explore the potential of this paradigm, we must also confront the challenges and risks that come with it. The choices we make today will shape the future of Bitcoin and the broader financial system for generations to come.

In conclusion, Bitcoin's journey is far from over. It has already achieved what many thought was impossible, and its potential to reshape the world of finance remains immense. Whether Bitcoin becomes the foundation of a new world currency or serves as a catalyst for further innovation, its legacy as a transformative force in the digital age is secure. The future of money is being written today, and Bitcoin is at the forefront of that story.